Multimedia Broadcasting and Multicasting in Mobile Networks

Multimedia Broadcasting and Multicasting in Mobile Networks

Grzegorz Iwacz
AGH University of Science and Technology, Poland

Andrzej Jajszczyk
AGH University of Science and Technology, Poland

Michał Zajączkowski
Comarch SA, Poland

WILEY

A John Wiley and Sons, Ltd, Publication

Registered office
John Wiley & Sons Ltd, The Atrium, Southern Gate, Chichester, West Sussex, PO19 8SQ,
United Kingdom

For details of our global editorial offices, for customer services and for information about
how to apply for permission to reuse the copyright material in this book please see our
website at www.wiley.com.

Library of Congress Cataloging-in-Publication Data

Iwacz, Grzegorz.
 Multimedia broadcasting and multicasting in mobile networks / Grzegorz
 Iwacz, Andrzej Jajszczyk, Michal Zajaczkowski.
   p. cm.
 Includes bibliographical references and index.
 ISBN 978-0-470-69686-6 (cloth)
 1. Multimedia communications—Congresses. 2. Computer networks—Congresses.
 I. Jajszczyk, Andrzej. II. Zajaczkowski, Michal. III. Title.
 TK5105.15.I83 2008
 384.3'3—dc22
                                                    2008017686

A catalogue record for this book is available from the British Library.

ISBN 978-0-470-69686-6 (HB)

Set in 11/13pt Sabon by Integra Software Services Pvt. Ltd, Pondicherry, India
Printed in Singapore by Markono Print Media Pte Ltd

To my great brother
Grzegorz Iwacz

To my wife Basia
Andrzej Jajszczyk

To my beloved wife Małgosia and to my parents
Michał Zajączkowski

Contents

About the Authors   xi

Abbreviations and Acronyms   xiii

List of Figures   xix

List of Tables   xxiii

1 Introduction   1
    References   4

2 Multicast   5
    2.1   The Idea of Multicast   7
    2.2   Justifying the Cost of Multicast   9
    2.3   Drawbacks of Multicast   13
    2.4   IP Multicast   16
          2.4.1   IP Multicast Networking Procedure   18
          2.4.2   Mobility of Users   21
    References   22

3 Internet Protocol Datacasting   23
    3.1   System Architecture   25
    3.2   Digital Video Broadcasting   28
          3.2.1   DVB-T as a Basis for DVB-H   29
          3.2.2   Digital Video Broadcasting Handheld   30
    3.3   Electronic Service Guide   40
    3.4   Streaming   43
    3.5   Data Transmission   46
    3.6   Interaction Channel   48
    References   51

4   **Multimedia Broadcast/Multicast Service (MBMS)**   **55**
    4.1   MBMS Overview   56
    4.2   MBMS Architecture   59
    4.3   MBMS Services   65
    4.4   Performance of MBMS   68
    References   69

5   **Alternative Technologies**   **71**
    5.1   MediaFLO   71
          5.1.1   Architecture   72
          5.1.2   System Performance   73
          5.1.3   Technical Description   74
          5.1.4   Summary   77
    5.2   Digital Multimedia Broadcasting (DMB)   78
          5.2.1   Multiplexing and Channel Coding   82
          5.2.2   Modulation and Transmission   86
          5.2.3   Summary   88
    5.3   Terrestrial Integrated Services Digital
          Broadcasting (ISDB-T)   88
          5.3.1   Overview of ISDB-T   89
          5.3.2   ISDB-T Transmission System   90
          5.3.3   Summary   97
    5.4   Comparison of Technologies   97
    References   99

6   **Digital Rights Management (DRM)**   **101**
    6.1   OMA DRM v2.0   102
    6.2   Windows Media DRM 10   105
    6.3   IPsec   106
    6.4   Secure Real-Time Transport Protocol   108
    6.5   ISMACrypt   110
    6.6   DVB Conditional Access   111
    6.7   Limitations of DRM Systems   112
    References   114

7   **Business Model**   **115**
    7.1   Common Components   116
    7.2   Components Specific to IPDC   119
    7.3   Components Specific to MBMS   121
    7.4   Terminals and Network Infrastructure   123

7.5   Charging Scenarios   130
7.6   Spectrum for Mobile TV   132
7.7   Summary   138
References   138

8   Trials   141
8.1   DVB-H Trials   142
8.2   MBMS Trials   149
8.3   MediaFLO Trials   150
References   151

9   User Feedback   153
9.1   Interest   154
9.2   Threats   155
9.3   Business Issues   157
9.4   Usage Schemes   158
9.5   The User   161
9.6   Comparison of Services   163
9.7   Mobile TV and Interactivity   165
9.8   Summary   169
References   170

10   Conclusion   171

Further Reading   175

Index   177

About the Authors

Grzegorz Iwacz works in the Internet industry. His major interest is the development of web applications. He received his MS degree from AGH University of Science and Technology, Krakow, Poland (major: Telecommunications Networks and Services) in 2006. He also received a Bachelor's degree from Jagiellonian University, Krakow, Poland (major: Human–Computer Interaction) in 2008. He was a student at Helsinki University of Technology, Espoo, Finland in 2005 and was in touch with practical aspects of multicast, especially IPDC technology implementations, while visiting Finland in 2005 and 2006. He has a high level of interest in efficient multimedia delivery in mobile networks and has followed the IPDC technology since its early stages.

Andrzej Jajszczyk is a professor at AGH University of Science and Technology in Krakow, Poland. He received his MS, PhD, and Dr Hab. degrees from Poznan University of Technology in 1974, 1979 and 1986, respectively. He spent several years at universities in Australia and Canada. He is the author or co-author of six books and over 230 papers, as well as 19 patents in the areas of telecommunications switching, high-speed networking and network management. He has been a consultant to industry, telecommunications operators and government agencies. He was the Editor-in-Chief of *IEEE Communications Magazine* and also serves on the editorial boards of various reputed journals, including *Annales des Télécommunications*, *China Communications* and *Computer Communications*. Over many years he has been active in the IEEE Communications Society, where he is currently its Vice-President. He is a member of the Association of Polish Electrical Engineers and a Fellow of the IEEE.

Michał Zajączkowski is an OSS Solution Manager in the Telecommunications Business Unit at Comarch SA. He received his MS degree from AGH University of Science and Technology, Krakow, Poland (major: Telecommunications Networks and Services) in

2006. In 2005, while studying at Helsinki University of Technology, he had his first contact with the practical aspects of multicast. This was then followed by a thorough study on the subject of multicast-based technologies, such as IPDC and MBMS, from their very early standardization stages. The study was accompanied by subsequent visits to Finland, scheduled to meet with mobile operators as well as with research and standardization bodies.

Abbreviations and Acronyms

2k, 4k, 8k mode	COFDM operation modes
3GPP	Third Generation Partnership Project
AAC	Advanced Audio Coding
ACK	Acknowledgement
ADT	Application Data Table
AES	Advanced Encryption Standard
AH	Authentication Header
AKA	Authentication and Key Agreement
ALC/LCT	Asynchronous Layered Coding/Layered Coding Transport
ARIB	Association of Radio Industries and Businesses
AS	Autonomous System
ATSC	Advanced Television Systems Committee
AVC	Advanced Video Coding
BAN	Body Area Network
BIFS	Binary Format for Scenes
BM-SC	Broadcast/Multicast Service Center
BSAC	Bit-Sliced Arithmetic Coding
CA	Conditional Access
CB	Cell Broadcast
CBMS	Convergence of Broadcast and Mobile Services
CCK	Complementary Code Keying
CEK	Content Encryption Key
CIDR	Classless Inter-Domain Routing
CN	Core Network
C/N	Carrier-to-Noise
COFDM	Coded Orthogonal Frequency Division Multiplexing
CPU	Central Processing Unit
CRC	Cyclic Redundancy Check
CSMA/CA	Carrier Sense Multiple Access with Collision Avoidance
D/A	Digital to Analog Converter

DAB	Digital Audio Broadcasting
DCF	DRM Content Format
DCO	Datacast Operator
DMB	Digital Multimedia Broadcasting
DMFC	Direct Methanol Fuel Cell
DQPSK	Differential Quadrature Phase Shift Keying
DRM	Digital Rights Management
DSSS	Direct Sequence Spread Spectrum
DVB	Digital Video Broadcasting
DVB-H	Digital Video Broadcasting Handheld
DVB-S	Digital Video Broadcasting Satellite
DVB-T	Digital Video Broadcasting Terrestrial
EC	European Commission
EDGE	Enhanced Data rates for GSM Evolution
EDR	Event Detail Record
EHF	Extremely High Frequency
EIGRP	Enhanced Interior Gateway Routing Protocol
EPG	Electronic Program Guide
ES	Elementary Stream
ESG	Electronic Service Guide
ESP	Encapsulating Security Payload
ETSI	European Telecommunications Standards Institute
FCC	Federal Communications Commission
FDT	File Delivery Table
FEC	Forward Error Correction
FFT	Fast Fourier Transform
FHSS	Frequency Hopping Spread Spectrum
FIC	Fast Information Channel
FLO	Forward Link Only
FLUTE	File Delivery over Unidirectional Transport
Gbit	Gigabit
GERAN	GSM EDGE Radio Access Network
GGSN	GPRS Gateway Support Node
GPRS	General Packet Radio Service
GPS	Global Positioning System
GSM	Global System for Mobile communications
GTP	GPRS Tunneling Protocol
HDTV	High Definition Television
HF	High Frequency
HMAC-SHA1	Keyed Hashing for Message Authentication

HSDPA	High-Speed Downlink Packet Access
HTTP	Hypertext Transfer Protocol
IETF	Internet Engineering Task Force
IF	Intermediate Frequency
IFFT	Inverse Fast Fourier Transform
IGMP	Internet Group Management Protocol
IPDC	Internet Protocol Datacasting
IPsec	IP security
IR	Infrared
ISDB	Integrated Services Digital Broadcasting
ISDB-C	Integrated Services Digital Broadcasting Cable
ISDB-S	Integrated Services Digital Broadcasting Satellite
ISDB-T	Integrated Services Digital Broadcasting Terrestrial
ISM	Industrial, Scientific and Medical
ISMACrypt	Internet Streaming Media Alliance Encryption and Authentication
ISP	Internet Service Provider
IT	Information Technology
ITU-R	International Telecommunication Union – Radiocommunication Sector
ITU-T	International Telecommunication Union – Telecommunication Standardization Sector
KMM	Key Management Message
KSM	Key Stream Message
LCT	Layered Coding Transport
LF	Low Frequency
LOC	Local Operation Center
MAC	Medium Access Control
MBMS	Multimedia Broadcast/Multicast Service
MCI	Multiplex Configuration Information
MF	Medium Frequency
MFN	Multifrequency Network
MIMO	Multiple-Input Multiple-Output
MMS	Multimedia Messaging System
MOT	Multimedia Object Transfer
MPE	Multiprotocol Encapsulation
MPE-FEC	Forward Error Correction for Multiprotocol Encapsulated data
MPEG	Moving Picture Experts Group
MSC	Main Service Channel

NACK   Negative Acknowledgement
NAT   Network Address Translation
NOC   National Operations Center
NPAD   Non-Program-Associated Data
NRK   Norwegian Broadcasting Corporation
OFDM   Orthogonal Frequency Division Multiplexing
OFDMA   Orthogonal Frequency Division Multiple Access
OIS   Overhead Information Symbols
OMA   Open Mobile Alliance
PAD   Program-Associated Data
PC   Power Control
PSI/SI   Program-Specific Information/Service Information
PTMP   Point-to-Multipoint
QAM   Quadrature Amplitude Modulation
QoS   Quality of Service
QPSK   Quadrature Phase Shift Keying
RAN   Radio Access Network
REK   Rights Encryption Key
RF   Radio Frequency
RFID   Radio Frequency Identification
RMT   Reliable Multicast Transport
RNC   Radio Network Controller
RS   Reed–Solomon
RSC   Radio Spectrum Committee
RSPG   Radio Spectrum Policy Group
RTCP   Real-Time Control Protocol
RTP   Real-Time Transport Protocol
RTSP   Real-Time Streaming Protocol
S-DMB   Satellite Digital Multimedia Broadcasting
SA   Security Association
SAP   Session Announcement Protocol
SDP   Session Description Protocol
SDTV   Standard Definition Television
SDU   Service Data Unit
SFN   Single Frequency Network
SGSN   Serving GPRS Support Node
SHF   Super High Frequency
SIR   Signal-to-Interference Ratio
SMS   Short Message Service
SNR   Signal-to-Noise Ratio
SOC   Service Operation Center

SPI	Security Parameter Index
SPP	Service Purchase and Protection
SRTP	Secure Real-Time Transport Protocol
T-DMB	Terrestrial Digital Multimedia Broadcasting
TDD	Time Division Duplexing
TDM	Time Division Multiplexing
TDMA	Time Division Multiple Access
TMCC	Transmission and Multiplexing Configuration Control
TPS	Transmitter Parameter Signaling
TS	Transport Stream
UDP	User Datagram Protocol
UE	User Equipment
UHF	Ultra High Frequency
ULE	Ultra Lightweight Encapsulation
UMTS	Universal Mobile Telecommunications System
URL	Uniform Resource Locator
UTRAN	UMTS Terrestrial Radio Access Network
UWB	Ultra-Wideband
VHF	Very High Frequency
VLF	Very Low Frequency
VLSM	Variable Length Subnet Mask
VoD	Video-on-Demand
WAP	Wireless Application Protocol
WAPECS	Wireless Access Policy for Electronic Communications Services
WARC	World Administrative Radio Conference
WCDMA	Wideband Code Division Multiple Access
WEP	Wired Equivalent Privacy
WiBro	Wireless Broadband
WiMAX	Wireless Microwave Access
WLAN	Wireless Local Area Network
WMAN	Wireless Metropolitan Area Network
WPAN	Wireless Personal Area Network
WWAN	Wireless Wide Area Network
XML	Extensible Markup Language

List of Figures

2.1	Simplified data delivery scheme for the point-to-point approach	6
2.2	Simplified data delivery scheme for the broadcast technique	7
2.3	Multicast gain metric for up to 50 receivers	12
2.4	Multicast gain metric for up to 1000 receivers	12
2.5	Cost growth in relation to the number of users	13
2.6	Reference model of a generic end-to-end multicast system	17
2.7	Generalized procedure to provide and receive multicast services	19
2.8	IP multicast delivery techniques (a) IP routed; (b) IP switched by tunnel	20
3.1	DVB-H-enabled Nokia N77	24
3.2	Functional entities and their interrelations	25
3.3	Protocol hicrarchy in IP Datacast	27
3.4	Structure of a DVB-H receiver	32
3.5	A conceptual description of using the DVB-H system (shared multiplexer)	33
3.6	Possible network topology solutions for DVB-H	34
3.7	Principle of time slicing	35
3.8	Relationship between burst bitrate and power saving	35
3.9	Structure of the MPE-FEC frame	37
3.10	Functional block diagram of the DVB-H transmission system (affected blocks shaded)	39
3.11	Nokia ESG solution	40
3.12	ESG operation diagram	41
3.13	ESG structure	42
3.14	Basic protocol stack for content delivery (shaded elements responsible for data streaming)	44
3.15	Hypothetical receiver buffering model	45

3.16 Basic protocol stack for content delivery (shaded
     elements responsible for file delivery) 46
3.17 Architecture of FLUTE 47
3.18 Implementation of interaction channel 48
3.19 Broadcast mobile convergence (integrating
     broadcast with interactive) 51
4.1 Phases of MBMS service provisioning in the
     multicast and broadcast modes 58
4.2 Logical MBMS architecture designed by 3GPP 60
4.3 BM-SC functional structure 62
4.4 Comparison of MBMS with other media delivery
     approaches 68
5.1 FLO technology architecture with external content
     providers 72
5.2 FLO's air interface in relation to the OSI/ISO
     model 75
5.3 FLO super-frame structure 76
5.4 FLO transport protocol stack 76
5.5 DMB services 80
5.6 Video service multiplexing schema 81
5.7 Channel coding and multiplexing process 83
5.8 DMB transmission frame structure 85
5.9 Diagram of ISDB-T transmitter 91
5.10 Example of hierarchical transmission and partial
     reception (6 MHz system with 13 segments) 94
5.11 Channel coding diagram 95
5.12 Block diagram of OFDM modulation 96
6.1 OMA DRM functional architecture 103
6.2 IPsec Security Association elements 107
6.3 ISMACrypt key management 111
6.4 Fujitsu FOMA F905i mobile phone with an in-built
     fingerprint sensor 114
7.1 Generic business value chain 116
7.2 IPDC value chain 119
7.3 MBMS value chain 122
7.4 Success factors for future terminals 124
7.5 Nokia 7710 with DVB-H receiver 127
7.6 Nokia SU-33W DVB-H receiver 128
7.7 Mobile TV – use of spectrum 134
8.1 Nokia 7710 with DVB-H receiver 147
9.1 Percentage of users satisfied with the service 154

9.2   Mobile TV success factors   156
9.3   Percentage of customers eager to pay for the service   157
9.4   Service usage scenarios   158
9.5   Average service usage time per session   159
9.6   Average service usage time per day   159
9.7   Relationship between people's mood and the
       preferred type of entertainment   162
9.8   Division of users with respect to adoption of new
       services   163
9.9   Interest rates for various mobile TV services   163
9.10   Downlink data usage for various services   164
9.11   Comparison of mobile TV, traditional TV and radio
       in various contexts   165
9.12   Mobile TV evolution   167
9.13   Hybrid network architecture enabling interactive
       services for mobile TV   169

List of Tables

4.1 Typical MBMS services 66
5.1 Parameters of the transmission modes in DMB 87
5.2 ARIB standards for digital broadcasting 89
5.3 ISDB-T transmission schema 92
5.4 ISDB-T transmission modes 93
5.5 Comparison of multimedia delivery technologies 98
8.1 DVB-H-based trials (as of March 2008) 143

1

Introduction

We are currently witnessing an unbelievable technological development, some may even say a breakthrough. Over the last decade, the likes of DVD players, palmtops and, in particular, cell phones have become obvious everyday-use items. There has also been a rapid growth in the personal consumption of media. Services like pay-per-view and video-on-demand are becoming more and more common and are changing the way we look at multimedia – now users can choose whatever media they want, whenever and wherever they want.

The greatest phenomenon of all is an 'ordinary' cell phone. Alongside technological evolution, an amazing growth in mobile telephony has been experienced. The number of mobile subscribers reached over 3.3 billion by the end of November 2007 [1] and is predicted to rise to 4 billion by the end of 2008. If the growth rate remains at this level, we may anticipate around 6.2 billion mobile subscribers globally by 2011. This implies that around 94% of the world's population will be using a cell phone by then. Along with this, more than 1.15 billion cell phones were sold in 2007, with unit growth of around 12% expected in 2008, giving estimated sales figures of 1.29 billion units [2].

Over time, newer and newer features and additions have been introduced to the terminals. Vendors take part in a constant race to put new, more advanced and more capable cell phones on the market. So we get mobile terminals packed with technology that broadens their functionality. We can speak about convergence; one

Multimedia Broadcasting and Multicasting in Mobile Networks
G. Iwacz, A. Jajszczyk and M. Zajączkowski
© 2008 John Wiley & Sons, Ltd

single device may have all the additional functions, such as a camera, video camera, calendar, organizer, portable radio, music player, games console, GPS and, now, television. All of this automatically affects user demands concerning the services provided. The more functions are offered by the handhelds, the more advanced and sophisticated services are expected by the customers.

When we consider multimedia services (such as television, as mentioned previously, or large file downloads), we realize that the increasing traffic and congestion in the radio spectrum caused by these can lead to degradation of the quality of service. Providers have to live up to the users' expectations, offering rich, innovative, interactive services, but at the same time have to struggle to improve the user experience or at least keep it at the same, satisfying level. It quickly becomes obvious that the existing network technologies cannot handle this. We can compare this to the rapid growth of the number of Internet users in the mid-1990s. The network would have collapsed long ago by now if some measures had not been taken. New ideas and adjustments had to be implemented. Scientists came up with network technologies such as VLSM (Variable Length Subnet Mask), CIDR (Classless Inter-Domain Routing) and NAT (Network Address Translation) which helped to overcome the crisis and are now commonly used. Right now, however, the situation has pretty much gone full circle and implementation of new solutions is inevitable.

Let us get back to the television issue. When we consider a cell phone as a TV terminal, it becomes apparent that the place of viewing is no longer limited to the television set back at home or even in the car. Instead, personal viewing of television is possible at any time and in any place, which makes perfect sense since most of our time is spent away from home or traveling. It was cellular networks that brought television to handhelds. However, providing the service that way was expensive and proved unfeasible. 2.5G telephone technologies, such as EDGE General Packet Radio Service, may theoretically provide a maximum rate of 473 kbit/s, but using them for TV transmission certainly would not be cheap. What is more, content distribution is also expensive, as telephone networks use point-to-point connections. As a result, mobile telecommunication technology is mainly used for personal communication.

It would be much more effective to use a point-to-multipoint architecture. In other words, the answer to these problems is multicast. This addresses the idea that it is far more effective to deliver the content to users simultaneously using a shared multicast path. That way, the data transmissions are not duplicated. We can also consider this from another point of view. When we talk about television, we assume broadcast. And while mentioning mobiles, a natural successor here is multicast. Broadcast is not a good solution as we do not want to send the content to everyone, only to some group that has ordered it and is willing to pay for it. To sum up, multicast enables the distribution of multimedia content cheaply to large groups of users.

Currently, several initiatives are undergoing a process of constant development, standardization and commercialization. At the same time, they are competing to emerge as the dominant technology standard in mobile broadcast television. We believe that two of these technologies, IPDC (Internet Protocol Datacasting) and MBMS (Multimedia Broadcast/Multicast Service), are the leading broadcast contenders. Although these originate from different backgrounds – digital television and third-generation cellular networks – both promise to provide truly multicast (meaning point-to-multipoint) services. On the following pages we are going to present both technologies, albeit with a little weighting towards IPDC. We will also try to answer the question of what users think about the technology, these new possibilities and whether it will deliver the new *killer application*. Of course, the other competing technologies will also be discussed briefly.

The book is organized in the following way. This chapter gives a general overview of the book and also introduces the subject matter. Chapter 2 provides information about multicast in general, describing the common issues concerning the technologies mentioned later on. Chapter 3 focuses on IPDC, giving a thorough analysis of the architecture, technical details, capabilities, offered services, etc. Chapter 4 has a similar construction to Chapter 3 but in it we present MBMS. In Chapter 5 we will continue the technical discussion, evaluating selected alternative technologies. Next, Chapter 6 tackles an issue particularly important for all technologies, which is protecting the delivered content from unauthorized access. In other words, we will get in-depth insights into DRM (Digital Rights Management) systems. Following this, in Chapter 7, we will move to the business aspects of the technologies, discussing the most probable value chains and presenting all the parties engaged and the possible benefits for each of them. Here, we will also tackle the important issue of charging, including the proposed charging schemes. Then, Chapter 8 will take a closer look at some of the existing implementations of the technologies and also ongoing trials. Chapter 9 will be a summary of our market research, focused on evaluating the acceptance of the new services, costs that the customers are willing to indulge and the best-acknowledged form. Finally, Chapter 10 serves as the conclusion of the book, summarizing the main aspects covered.

REFERENCES

[1] 'Global cellphone penetration reaches 50 pct,' Reuters UK, 26 November 2007, http://investing.reuters.co.uk/news/articleinvesting. aspx?type=media&storyID=nL29.

[2] D. Ford, J. Rebello and T. Teng, Mobile Handset Market Tracker, iSuppli, 2008.

2

Multicast

At the beginning of this chapter we will briefly present the point-to-point transmission concept. After that, broadcast and multicast techniques will be described. A comparison of these methods will be followed by a presentation of the advantages and disadvantages of each. After that it will become clear that multicast is the right and suitable choice for multimedia delivery. At the end, we will introduce IP multicast as a practical application of the described multicast transmission concept.

Currently, most mobile communication standards are based on the point-to-point transmission method. GSM and UMTS networks use this kind of communication to provide a variety of services including voice calls and Internet access. A simplified network structure presenting the principle of unicast is shown in Figure 2.1.

Every single user is handled by the network individually. All the communication and requested data are transmitted to each user separately. What if all devices require the same content at the same time? In the unicast scenario, where all receivers use dedicated network resources, the same information is sent to every single user in parallel. Of course, this situation leads to inefficient usage of core network resources. This is even more critical if we consider the radio interface, where the bandwidth is limited and should be utilized with care. Furthermore, every terminal within

Multimedia Broadcasting and Multicasting in Mobile Networks
G. Iwacz, A. Jajszczyk and M. Zajączkowski
© 2008 John Wiley & Sons, Ltd

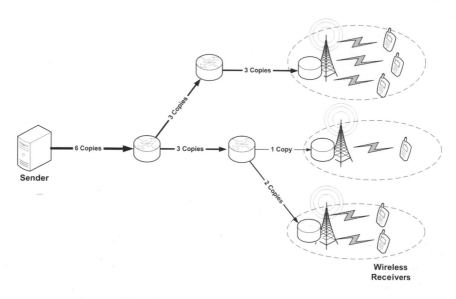

Figure 2.1 Simplified data delivery scheme for the point-to-point approach

the transmitter's range is able to receive the data. As multimedia services consume a lot of network resources, the number of users able to access such services in a unicast manner is highly limited.

A solution to this problem could be a system transmitting the data through the network only once instead of sending multiple copies of the same content. This would provide access to the service for a practically unlimited number of users. The described situation appears in broadcast networks and an example would be terrestrial television. A simple illustration of the operation of a broadcast network is shown in Figure 2.2. As we can see, only a single instance of the data is transmitted through the network, including the radio link, and only a single instance is processed by the nodes. This is a very effective means of transmission when group communication is considered.

However, this scenario has a significant disadvantage in that it is relevant only if all the users are interested in the broadcast data. This problem is addressed by multicast, which is the best solution if the content is destined only for a certain group of users. Transmission of confidential or copyrighted content is a good example.

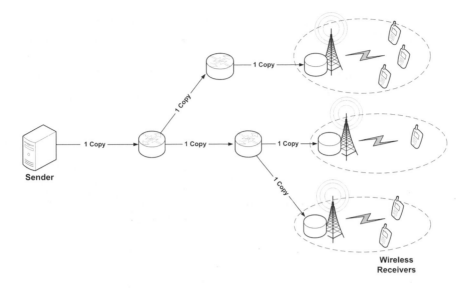

Figure 2.2   Simplified data delivery scheme for the broadcast technique

2.1   THE IDEA OF MULTICAST

We describe multicast as the simultaneous delivery, or communication, of data between several parties. Point-to-multipoint communication is one particular form and the main topic of this book. However, we need to realize that multicast also covers multipoint-to-multipoint and multipoint-to-point communication. Considering the communication model, the following approaches exist [1]:

- **Application layer multicast:** the same content or data is delivered to a group of applications using point-to-point connections. It only provides a simultaneous flow of information and does not increase efficiency in network usage since unicast is still used. Email with multiple recipients is a good example.
- **Network layer multicast:** while sending the same data to a group of users, the network optimizes routing to send this data through a link only once instead of sending it to every single user separately. Thus, data duplication is required only if some recipients are reachable via different links. This type of delivery increases efficiency in network usage and provides simultaneous data delivery.

- **Physical layer multicast:** the same signal is transmitted via a physical link. Broadcast in the Ethernet is an appropriate example.

The most significant subclass is the network layer multicast. Only this scenario provides increased efficiency in group communication and offers benefits to multimedia transmissions. Another division worth mentioning concerns user–network communication:

- **Active:** the receiving entity is active, which means it is able to communicate with the network via an uplink channel. Thus, it is able to launch a request for the service. A return channel does not need to be in the same network as the downlink – the receiver may communicate with the sender using a return channel of some other network.
- **Passive:** the receiving entity does not have an uplink channel – it cannot communicate with the network. In order to equip the receiver with the possibility of service selection, the sender is obliged to add some service information to the provided data.

Multicast with passive user-network communication is scalable. Unfortunately, the return path signaling reduces scalability and increases complexity. However, it increases reliability and security and enables collection of usage reports. Both of these subclasses have pros and cons and are widely used in multicast technology.

The means of delivering content is another matter to consider. Two major delivery scenarios can be distinguished as follows:

- **Real-time:** the data stream is provided in real time to all users in a multicast group simultaneously, without significant delays or jitter, although data loss may occur. This type of delivery applies to services where timely delivery is a key factor, rather than reliable delivery. Videoconferencing is the most relevant example.
- **Reliable:** the network guarantees reliability of the transmitted data, thus some delays may occur. File downloading is a simple example of such a service.

Some other types are available; however, these two seem to be most often deployed in practice. The data delivery method depends largely on user habits and service or application requirements.

Of all the presented divisions, in this book we deal with point-to-multipoint, network layer, active and passive multicast. Moreover, we discuss various types of data delivery techniques, especially real-time content delivery and reliable transmission.

2.2 JUSTIFYING THE COST OF MULTICAST

As the available bandwidth increases in the last mile, so does the traffic in the backbone. Users are aware of the possibility of accessing new, multimedia-oriented services and are generating more and more traffic. Simultaneous service usage is a very common situation when multimedia-rich services are considered, thus using point-to-point technology in this case causes unnecessary multiplication of relatively bandwidth-consuming data streams. The point-to-multipoint communication model is an intuitive solution. However, since intuition is not always sufficient, we will provide some simple analytical assessment to justify the multicast-based solution. A relatively simple metric was necessary to evaluate multicast effectiveness, a metric representing some degree of accuracy and general enough to be relevant to the vast majority of network topologies.

So where exactly does the multicast gain come from? First of all, a source issues only a single packet irrespective of the number of receivers, which reduces the impact on local bandwidth and server resources. Secondly, the network replicates the packet only when the paths to the receiver diverge. Each link carries one copy of the multicast packet, while the quantity of unicast packets equals the number of receivers: the efficiency is proportional to the number of downstream receivers.

We also have to ask who, and in what way, will benefit from using multicast? We can distinguish the following three main groups of beneficiaries:

- **End-users:** these are not concerned about a possible gain, all they care about is the availability of services, the quality and the cost; the delivery technique is not important.
- **Service providers:** they worry about the impact of increased service usage and traffic in their networks on local resources (servers, LANs).
- **Network providers:** they have to ensure that their own resources (routers, high-speed links) are used as efficiently as possible.

The common factor across the above-mentioned interests is bandwidth. And it is exactly on bandwidth that the metric proposed by R. Chalmers and K. Almeroth is based [2]. The metric compares the total number of links traversed by multicast and unicast packets over a given topology:

$$\delta = 1 - \frac{L_m}{L_u} \qquad (2.1)$$

where

  L_m is the total number of multicast links in the distribution link
  L_u is the total number of unicast hops (counting duplicate packets)

By δ we denote the percentage gain in the bandwidth utilization achieved by using multicast rather than unicast. The multicast metric is a fraction in the range $0 \leq \delta \leq 1$. When the value equals zero, there is no difference in the number of hops. Growth in the metric indicates higher efficiency gains when using multicast.

It is really hard to determine the hop count for both unicast and multicast traffic accurately for a real multicast group. A number of factors that will be mentioned later can significantly complicate the matter. That is why a simplified approach was proposed: it is assumed that multicast and unicast paths are identical. Even with regard to the simplified approach, it is impossible to count the group members without using some kind of sophisticated tool. D. Makofske and K. Almeroth proposed *MHealth* [3]. The *Multicast Health Monitor* gathers information about each source and receiver in a multicast group and then determines the paths between them. It uses the RTCP (Real-Time Control Protocol) feedback to determine each of the sources and receivers. Consequently, the hop counts can be computed.

As mentioned before, there are some problems with this approach. Below, some of the used assumptions are discussed:

- **Multicast tunnels:** multicast routes traverse tunnels, but the unicast routers present in the tunnels are not reported by current tracing utilities. The model implicitly assumes that no tunnels exist in the multicast tree. This lowers the measured metric since duplicate unicast streams do not contribute their full cost when tunnels shorten their logical paths.

- **Multi-access links:** *MHealth* does not identify multi-access links and falsely assumes that each link is point-to-point. Ignoring shared links results in a worst case view of the multicast efficiency.
- **Dynamic membership:** new sources and receivers can join the group at any time. On the other hand, the method works on a snapshot of the multicast network made sequentially and, for example, some receivers that join only for a short period of time may be missed.
- **Dial-up links:** these degrade the multicast to unicast on the last hop.

Let us get back to the metric. J. Chuang and M. Sirbu in their work [4] proposed a cost function which is closely related to the earlier presented metric and defines a direct relationship between the hop counts and the group size:

$$\frac{L_m}{\overline{L_u}} = N^k \tag{2.2}$$

where

L_m is the total length of the multicast distribution tree
$\overline{L_u}$ is the average unicast routing path length
N is the multicast group size
k is the economies of scale factor (for most topologies $k \approx 0.8$).

Now assuming $\overline{L_u} = \dfrac{L_u}{N}$ we get:

$$\delta = 1 - N^\varepsilon \tag{2.3}$$

where

$\varepsilon = k - 1 \approx 0.8 - 1 \approx -0.2$ (efficiency factor).

Equation (2.3) provides us with an estimate for the multicast efficiency that depends only on the number of receivers in the multicast group. Figures 2.3 and 2.4 present the function for 50 and 1000 receivers with a few values of ε.

With even a small number of receivers, multicast outperforms unicast by a wide margin. For 20 to 40 receivers, we can expect a 60–70% increase in efficiency, reaching 80% for 150 receivers [5].

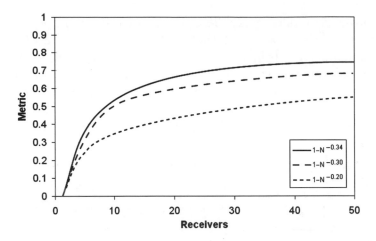

Figure 2.3 Multicast gain metric for up to 50 receivers [5]

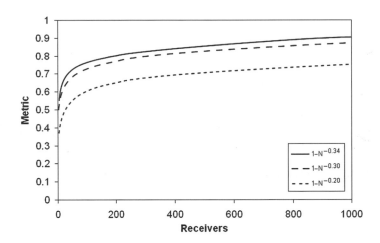

Figure 2.4 Multicast gain metric for up to 1000 receivers [5]

To summarize, today multicast makes sense for an ISP or corporate customer only when the bandwidth savings are higher than the deployment and management costs. B. Cain from Nortel Networks suggests this is multicast deployment's *sweet spot* [6]. The sweet spot is where the additional cost of providing the service is outweighed by the gained performance benefit. Figure 2.5 illustrates this principle.

The cost of a network service can be defined as the sum of the network-related costs (router state processing and signaling,

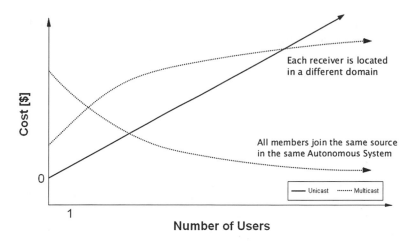

Figure 2.5 Cost growth in relation to the number of users [6]

inter-domain routing scalability) and management costs (ease of deployment and maintenance). As illustrated in Figure 2.5, unicast is represented as a rising straight line because each new receiver adds a new cost (mostly network cost). Multicast, however, has a high initial cost which is higher than unicast.

In the best case, it is advantageous to use multicast over unicast services for low numbers of receivers (downward-sloping dotted line). This corresponds to a group where all members would join the same source in the same AS (autonomous system).

Less optimistically (upward-sloping dotted line), multicast requires a larger receiver set (that might be an order of magnitude larger compared to the optimistic case) before a benefit over unicast becomes apparent. This, however, corresponds to the scenario where each additional multicast receiver may exist in a different domain [6].

2.3 DRAWBACKS OF MULTICAST

Multicast disadvantages emerge from sharing the data with more than one recipient. Cost distribution, intellectual rights, security, management – all of these are quite different and more troublesome than in the unicast scenario. For example, the functionalities mentioned above are divided between scenario actors and depend on application type. Some major IP multicast drawbacks are related to the following issues [6]:

- group management;
- security;
- billing;
- address allocation;
- network management;
- additional services.

We define group management as a set of access control functions determining who can be a transmitter and who can join a multicast group (who can receive a particular service). It basically consists of the following functions: receiver authorization and authentication as well as transmission authorization. The lack of this component in the IP multicast model can be troublesome for end-users as well as for service providers. In a particular case, unauthorized reception of data like *pay-per-content* is possible, while every user can enter a group without any authorization. This causes revenue loss for content providers and may even lead to shutting down the service. Moreover, some information can be stolen this way.

A more fundamental concern in group management is content provider recognition. Unauthorized providers may flood a network with useless data, causing congestion, data loss or even network collapse. Moreover, they can even imitate some authentic content source. An example here would be a fake web page for a bank, used to obtain access credentials such as usernames and passwords (phishing and pharming). IGMP (Internet Group Management Protocol) version 3 could be an answer to some of these management faults. It basically prunes data sources, denying unauthorized data entry to the backbone and enabling source-specific joining. However, in some scenarios, there is still a threat of attack even while using the IGMPv3 protocol.

Another significant drawback is the lack of proper security in the system. This matter is strictly related to group management weaknesses: problems with authentication and authorization provide a wide open backdoor for hackers. Thanks to IPsec (IP security standard), a receiver has the ability to prune data streams from unauthorized senders. End-to-end encryption at the application layer is often used as a mechanism to provide data privacy, solving the authentication and authorization problems at some point.

While heterogeneous group key management is required, the scalability problem appears. Therefore, rekeying on portions of the tree is necessary, but with this approach the system complexity increases. On the other hand, the network-level approach is possible. Appropriate protocols assure access to the multicast tree only for known and authorized hosts. These application-level and network-level mechanisms are a partial solution for providing data integrity.

Another security issue is the location of the access lists, i.e. the lists of authorized receivers. Two approaches are possible: focused either at source or at dedicated authentication servers. Security solutions add complexity to the model, making some processes more time consuming. This causes the model to be at odds with application requirements, like fast join and other time-relevant mechanisms.

Billing in an IP multicast model is another relevant issue. Nowadays, multicast helps in efficient network utilization and it is beneficial for the content provider rather than the customer. The reason for this is a relatively complicated charging and billing mechanism that is much more complex than in the unicast scenario. Since the service is addressed to a group, multicast tree costs and savings must be divided between group members. Moreover, cost distribution is even more complicated when the QoS requirements of group participants differ.

The quality demands of the application layer, costs and savings of multicast delivery are all relevant features in charging mechanisms if a usage-based approach is considered [7]. Flat-rate charging is an alternative and, thanks to its simplicity, seems to be a more attractive solution.

The current IPv4-based multicast address space is unregulated; there is no control over address allocation. More than one group can be assigned a single multicast address. Therefore, groups with the same address will receive each other's data. This problem concerns the receiver while it has to process and drop unwanted data. The probability of such a 'collision' is pretty high in the IPv4-based address space. Among many proposed solutions, IPv6 addressing seems to work best, as here the probability of collision is relatively low (less than $10^{-24}\%$).

Let us list some extra services that multicast could and should provide [6]:

- **Congestion control:** lack of this feature can be really harmful to well-behaving TCP connections.

- **Network performance measurement:** applications could adjust to network conditions.
- **Low-latency interdomain routing:** latency is relevant in this matter.
- **Unidirectional links:** multicast should be able to provide unidirectional communication.
- **Subcasting:** this is useful for receiver scooping [8] and is used by many congestion control and reliability protocols, e.g., RTP.
- **Service Level Agreement and Virtual Private Network management.**

2.4   IP MULTICAST

So far we have compared point-to-point and point-to-multipoint transmission techniques. This was accompanied by discussing some details concerning multicast. Now we will introduce IP multicast as a practical application of the multicast transmission concept.

Both systems mentioned in the Introduction, IPDC and MBMS, which will be described in detail in the following chapters, utilize the IP multicast IETF specifications. Although, as we have said, their background is different (digital television and third-generation cellular networks), they share some common system aspects. Both also treat IP multicast as a means of providing a unidirectional radio downlink.

Figure 2.6 shows a reference model of a generic end-to-end multicast system [9]. The main purpose here is to present the principal entities and interfaces.

The presented architecture is divided into the '3 Cs' business approach:

- **Content:** includes content and service delivery. Traditionally, the parties involved in this layer are content providers and aggregators.
- **Connection:** includes core and access networks operated by network operators.
- **Consumption:** includes user end equipment – client platforms and applications provided by hardware and software vendors.

One has to remember that, although each architectural layer is seen as a single component, it can consist of multiple physical

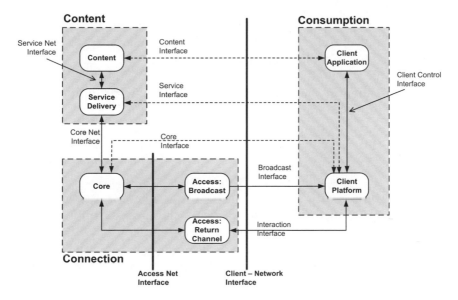

Figure 2.6 Reference model of a generic end-to-end multicast system [9]

and logical components. The following logical interfaces exist: the content interface (provides delivery of the content and its description), the service interface (offers services like streaming, reliability, billing, DRM – Digital Rights Management) and the core interface (guarantees Quality of Service, IP address assignment) [9].

Right now let us focus on the content delivery. The following three general platforms are required for provision of higher-level services in a multicast system:

- **Streaming:** used naturally for streaming of data from local storage or live sources. The most important issue here is timely delivery rather than perfect reliability. Available transmission rates, varying from tens of kilobits to several megabits per second, enable rich media services such as audio and video streaming to be served to large audiences simultaneously. Providing mobile television is an example here.

  Real-Time Transport Protocol (RTP) delivery is becoming the de facto choice for streaming transport. Related protocols, such as the Real-Time Control Protocol (RTCP, part of the same standard as RTP) and Real-Time Streaming Protocol (RTSP) provide additional features to a subset of applications.

- **Filecast:** meant for the simultaneous distribution of files. Here, many applications require a certain level of reliability, thus there is a need for reliable multicast protocols.

  Efforts to standardize Reliable Multicast Transport (RMT) have resulted in the IETF chartering a working group on RMT to produce, amongst other things, specifications that meet the reliable unidirectional delivery requirements [10].
- **Media discovery:** services as well as content are announced in advance and also during the session that delivers them. Thanks to this, users can choose particular services and access them at a chosen time.

  Generally, media are described by using a description syntax and semantics, such as Session Description Protocol (SDP), and delivered by using one or more transport protocols, such as Session Announcement Protocol (SAP) or even Hypertext Transfer Protocol (HTTP) [1].

2.4.1   IP Multicast Networking Procedure

Some general steps are required to provide and receive wireless multicast services. They are presented in Figure 2.7. The stages in dashed-line boxes are optional but widely used.

The presented steps can be described as follows [1]:

- Creation of content and then simple as well as complex services result in a ready source of content in formats compatible with the user equipment capabilities.
- The scheduling and agreements between network operators, intellectual rights owners and service aggregators have a basic impact on the technology.
- Service advertising may be out of band of the system (e.g., billboard advertising) or may be electronically available through web links or in-band service announcements.
- The registration may involve financial information exchange such as payment for subscriptions or authorizations to bill for services accessed later. If service media are to be secured (encrypted, authenticated, etc.), sufficient security information to access the media must either be given at registration or made available as a related service.
- Media discovery occurs as described earlier. Media discovery can also be out of band, using a dedicated point-to-point channel.

- On the network side, the backbone network infrastructure and the radio access network infrastructure must be configured.
- Protocols and technologies below the IP layer should be autonomous to obtain maximum interoperability of systems. This way, subsequent access by a user does not affect the higher-layer signaling. To ensure this, radio and link layer parameters can be signaled at the radio link in question. Multicast systems provide their own access-specific signaling to allow user devices to correctly associate radio and link channels with specific multicast services [1].

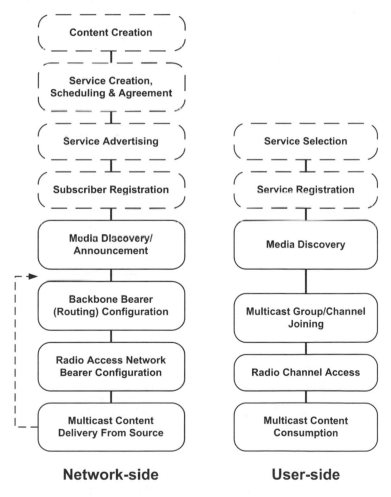

Figure 2.7   Generalized procedure to provide and receive multicast services [1]

There are many protocols that can be used to route and switch IP
multicast packets on the Internet. These include the option of tunneling multicast streams within unicast streams over one or more
links (where IP routed multicast is not feasible). Figures 2.8(a)
and 2.8(b) illustrate the essential difference between routed and
tunneled multicast.

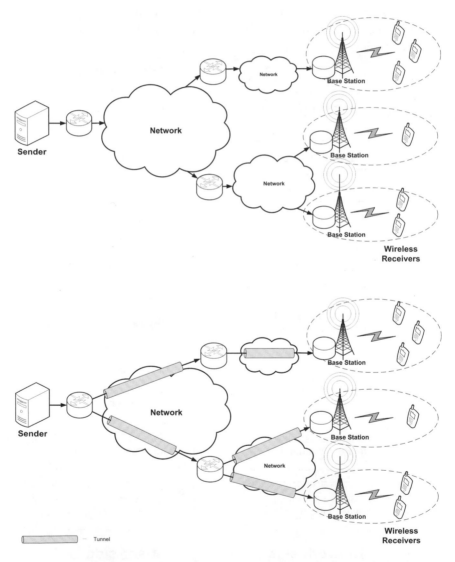

Figure 2.8 IP multicast delivery techniques (a) IP routed [1]; (b) IP switched by
tunnel [1]

Considering these figures, some issues are worth mentioning:

- tunnels add complexity;
- tunnels may cause duplicate data on the same link;
- tunnels guarantee that data pass through certain control points.

2.4.2 Mobility of Users

Content delivery to mobiles employs some wireless radio techniques. That is why we have to address the issue of the mobility of users. In consequence, two requirements arise: constant as well as independent-of-place access to the network services and consistent service as users are moving.

The first need is resolved thanks to wireless communications, but at the same time requires the device to be battery-powered. Thus, electrical consumption should be minimized whenever possible. This affects the physical design of the device as well as the protocols used. Features such as the device's ability to sleep – to shut down some internal circuits for some period of time – are crucial and must be implemented. Moreover, there should be a possibility to just passively receive data on the interface without an uplink channel. This issue will be described later.

As the users are moving most of the time, handovers are necessary. The service should also undergo a gentle degradation when it no longer can be maintained. Handover involves setting up new connections and releasing the old ones when the terminal moves from the radio coverage area of one cell to another.

Handover in wireless cellular systems is normally a three-phase process, consisting of:

1. Measurement (measurement criteria, measurement reports).
2. Decision (algorithm parameters, handover criteria).
3. Execution (handover signaling, radio resource allocation).

We also distinguish two types of handovers for the multicast service: active and passive. As the name implies, the active handover requires some action on the receiver side (specific signaling using the uplink). On the other hand, handover signaling forces the network to give sufficient information on the downlink for a user device to get the service in the new cell (no uplink signaling).

Another issue is that when talking about wireless communication, we have to remember the errors in radio transmission. Generally, the following two methods are used:

- increased coding of data to provide redundant information (FEC – Forward Error Correction);
- retransmission of data when loss is detected (we can use NACKs – Negative Acknowledgments, which scale much better in a one-to-many scenario than ACKs – Acknowledgments).

REFERENCES

[1] S. Dixit and T. Wu, *Content Networking In The Mobile Internet*, John Wiley & Sons, Inc., 2004.

[2] R. Chalmers and K. Almeroth, 'Developing a Multicast Metric,' in *Proceedings of IEEE Globecom 2000*, San Francisco, California, USA, December 2000.

[3] D. Makofske and K. Almeroth, 'MHealth: A real-time graphical multicast monitoring tool,' in *Proceedings of Workshop on Network and Operating System Support for Digital Audio and Video (NOSSDAV'99)*, Basking Ridge, New Jersey, USA, June 1999.

[4] J. Chuang and M. Sirbu, 'Pricing multicast communication: A cost based approach,' in *Proceedings of INET'98*, Geneva, Switzerland, July 1998.

[5] R. Chalmers and K. Almeroth, *A Characterization of Multicast Efficiency*, http://www.nmsl.cs.ucsb.edu/mwalk/metric.html, 10 December 2005.

[6] C. Diot, B. N. Levine, B. Lyles, H. Kassem and D. Balensiefen, 'Deployment Issues for the IP Multicast Service and Architecture,' *IEEE Network*, January 2000.

[7] G. Carle, F. Hartanto, M. Smirnov and T. Zseby, *Charging and accounting for QOS-enhanced IP multicast*, GMD Fokus, Germany.

[8] B. N. Levine, J. Crowcroft, C. Diot, J. J. Garcia-Luna-Aceves and J. F. Kurose, 'Consideration of Receiver Interest in Content for IP Delivery,' *Proceedings IEEE Infocom*, Tel Aviv, Israel, 26–30 March 2000.

[9] Sonera MediaLab White Paper, *IP Datacasting Content Services*, 2003.

[10] Reliable Multicast Transport IETF Working Group, *Working Group Charter*, http://www.ietf.org/html.charters/rmt-charter, 5 January 2006.

3

Internet Protocol Datacasting

Mobile phones are not used only for talking these days. Now they are
equipped with memory cards and large screens capable of displaying millions of colors, they have become multimedia devices. This
situation has pushed network operators to provide more and more
multimedia-based services like MMS (Multimedia Messaging System), Internet access and videocall via the UMTS (Universal Mobile
Telecommunications System) network, etc. We can listen to the
radio, mp3s or even read the news using our cell phone – it seems to
incorporate all the possible media services. And what about motion-
picture-based services? We could say that video streaming over 3G
networks is a relevant example, but to be honest, its quality and price
does not make it attractive. There is a need for a technology suitable
for providing high quality audio/video transmission to complete the
scope of multimedia services in handheld devices.

The audio/video transmission itself is not a problem; what then
is? Why can't we provide that kind of service? The main concept
of the existing networks is the answer. The cellular architecture
causes radio bandwidth limitations, which is an important issue here.
Moreover, batteries in mobile devices seem to be another problem –
constant radio receiver usage generates high power consumption and
causes fast battery exhaustion.

It is not easy to address these issues because, as we have said,
the problems concern the cellular architecture of today's mobile networks. Thus, the only possibility when it comes to providing the
discussed services is to propose a conceptually different network

Multimedia Broadcasting and Multicasting in Mobile Networks
G. Iwacz, A. Jajszczyk and M. Zajączkowski
© 2008 John Wiley & Sons, Ltd

infrastructure. For that reason, Internet Protocol Datacasting (IPDC) is being developed. It carries IP datagrams over a broadcast network, thus it is suitable for transmitting any data, not just high quality audio/video streams. However, television is our main interest, because IPDC is dedicated to it and because of the importance of the TV market – it is, for instance, much bigger than the telephony market.

Thanks to the DVB-H (Digital Video Broadcasting Handheld) standard, it is possible to transmit data at a rate of 22 Mbit/s. This is enough to provide over 50 high quality TV channels. This technology moves TV from our living room to our pockets (Figure 3.1) and gives us the possibility of watching it anywhere we want.

Figure 3.1 DVB-H-enabled Nokia N77 (reproduced by permission of © 2008 Nokia Corporation)

In this chapter our main concern is to present the IPDC technology in detail, which will be achieved by giving a thorough analysis of its main building blocks. To begin with, we describe the system architecture with some help from the OSI/ISO layer model and then present the main components of the system. Then we move on to DVB-H, which is the basis for the IPDC technology. After a thorough analysis of DVB-H we will provide some information about other components of the system: the Electronic Service Guide, audio/video compression, file delivery and the uplink communication channel will be covered in detail. All business aspects and implementation issues will be covered in the following chapters.

3.1   SYSTEM ARCHITECTURE

To begin with we shall describe the functional entities of the system and then we will focus on the protocol stack. Figure 3.2 shows the parts of the system and their interrelations (described later in the text).

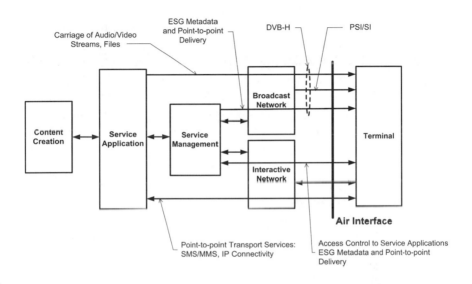

Figure 3.2   Functional entities and their interrelations [1]

In order to enable any multimedia services, first we need a primary source. Thus, the Content Creation block is the start element of the system in our model – the element responsible for content provisioning. And while the technology is based on Internet Protocol, the content can be of any kind, provided it fits into IP packets. Moreover, to distinguish services, it is obligatory to include the basic service description.

The Content Creation element is strictly connected to the Service Application module, which gathers data along with the related metadata from various Content Creation elements, offering them to users. It also has some security features; it is responsible for coding and service metadata provisioning to the Electronic Service Guide

(ESG). An important part of this module is the point of interaction with end terminals. This basically enables uplink communication and, in this way, also interactivity. There can be as many Service Application entities as there are services provided by IPDC.

The next part of the system is responsible for Service Management and can be divided into the following four functional entities:

- **Service Configuration and Resource Allocation:** this takes care of bandwidth allocation for Service Applications and binding a service to localization.
- **Service Guide Provisioning Application:** its main role is ESG aggregation from different Service Application entities. There can be more than one application in the Service Management module.
- **Security/Service Protection Provision:** its role is access control and management.
- Some location services can be provided to the Service Application module by the Service Management module.

The module responsible for security is of primary importance. The main IPDC feature, as we are transmitting over a broadcast network, is that the signal can be received by every user in the transmitter area. This means that even unauthorized terminals can receive the signal. If any user has access to every service, non-free services are useless. Therefore, an appropriate security system (Digital Rights Management) is important. We will cover this issue in more detail in Chapter 6.

The next module, the Broadcast Network, has two main features. First of all, it is responsible for multiplexing various Service Applications. Secondly, it handles security issues. However, when discussing the Broadcast Network module, the most important aspect to mention is the DVB-H-based data broadcast. It offers many improvements for data transmission to mobile devices, time slicing and encapsulation in particular. Thanks to this, terminal battery consumption is reduced, making the service attractive since the user does not need to recharge the terminal so often.

The Interactive Network is another element in the discussed architecture. As the name implies, it is a network element that enables terminal interaction with the system by providing an uplink connection to Service Application and Service Management entities. However, it is possible that some of the mentioned architecture elements do not enable such functionality. In this case, any interaction is impossible. Generally, interaction is a welcome feature. It increases security and makes new services possible [1].

A *terminal* may be any device capable of receiving, decoding and launching services provided by the other system entities. One of the terminals available commercially in Europe is shown in Figure 3.1. All the elements described above will be introduced in Chapter 7 in the form of a service value chain.

DVB-H, as a broadcast technology, does not provide any interactivity; there is no uplink communication in the standard. Content provision is not a matter either. Thus, the Content Provision and Interaction modules are not part of the DVB-CBMS (Convergence of Broadcast and Mobile Services) specification. Every other entity is within the scope of DVB-CBMS.

Now we will focus on the protocol stack. Figure 3.3 shows the protocol stack on a layered diagram.

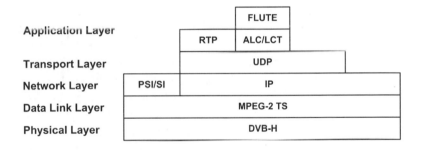

FLUTE: File Delivery over Unidirectional transport
RTP: Real-time Transport Protocol
ALC/LCT: Asynchronous Layered Coding/Layered Coding Transports
PSI/SI: Program Specific Information/Service Information
TS: Transport Stream

Figure 3.3 Protocol hierarchy in IP Datacast [1]

The general idea is to use a digital television broadcast network to transmit the data. DVB-H was developed especially for this purpose. As it is a digital television standard, it provides transmission based on the MPEG-2 (Moving Picture Experts Group) stream. Not just audio or video but any data can be encapsulated into the MPEG-2 transport stream and broadcast through a DVB network.

One of the advantages of the described technology is that it uses Internet Protocol. Everything that can be encapsulated into IP packets can be transmitted over the described network, as this is a common transmission protocol. Internet Protocol along with UDP (User Datagram Protocol) is responsible for data transmission, while PSI/SI (Program Specific Information/Service Information) is used for DVB signaling.

Two protocols are used in the application layer. FLUTE (File Delivery over Unidirectional Transport) is based on the ALC/LCT (Asynchronous Layered Coding/Layered Coding Transport) protocols. While FLUTE is designed for data transmission, RTP (Real-Time Transport Protocol) with RTCP (Real-Time Control Protocol) is used in the case of streaming.

3.2 DIGITAL VIDEO BROADCASTING

The key characteristic of IPDC is that it uses a digital television broadcast network as the physical carrier of the IP data. The reason for this is quite simple: with a broadcast network it costs the same amount of money to deliver services regardless of the number of users. Moreover, with broadcast transmission no bottlenecks exist.

Several digital television standards exist worldwide, such as ATSC (Advanced Television Systems Committee) in the United States, ISDB-T (Integrated Services Digital Broadcasting Terrestrial) in Japan and DVB (Digital Video Broadcasting) in Europe.

ATSC is a digital video broadcasting standard used in the United States and South Korea. It provides HDTV (High-Definition Television) services with fixed antenna reception. As a radio frequency modulation standard, the 8-level vestigial sideband (8-VSB) modulation is used. However, it is not suited for mobile or portable television reception and also has poor performance against the multipath effect.

The ISDB-T standard, developed and adopted in Japan, provides audio, video and multimedia services for the terrestrial television network. It accommodates HDTV as well as mobile reception as it is robust enough to handle the multipath fading interference. ISDB-T uses COFDM (Coded Orthogonal Frequency Division Multiplexing). Orthogonal frequency division multiplexing applied alongside convolutional coding for error protection enables undisturbed reception even under very difficult conditions. Also, thanks to the use of multiple carriers, the multipath effect is avoided. It is worth mentioning that ISDB-T supports time interleaving and the 4k modulation OFDM mode, which is particularly useful with mobile terminals.

DVB is the digital broadcasting standard adopted in Europe and is regulated by ETSI (European Telecommunications Standards Institute). It has many modalities, such as Satellite (DVB-S), Cable (DVB-C), Terrestrial (DVB-T) and, last but not least, Handheld (DVB-H).

In Europe, DVB-T (Digital Video Broadcasting for Terrestrial television) has been chosen as the standard for digital television to provide for portable and rooftop antenna reception. DVB-T has proven effective in meeting much more than its initial requirements; however, it still has some limitations in regard to mobile reception. On the basis of DVB-T, the DVB Project has developed a new standard: Digital Video Broadcasting Handheld (DVB-H), which is perfectly suitable for delivery of audio and video to mobile handheld devices. DVB-H overcomes the two main limitations of the DVB-T standard when used for handheld devices with build-in antennas by:

- lowering battery consumption;
- improving robustness in the very difficult environment of indoor and outdoor portable reception.

3.2.1 DVB-T as a Basis for DVB-H

DVB-T, the standard for terrestrial transmitters, was developed in 1997 by the DVB Project consortium. It has been adopted for providing digital television services in Europe. Each program here is sent by a separate logical channel, distinguished by a unique packet identifier.

DVB-T divides the signal into several thousand orthogonal subcarriers using COFDM. The transmission parameters are as follows:

- number of subcarriers;
- guard interval;
- channel bandwidth;
- modulation scheme.

The number of subcarriers affects the signal tolerance to the Doppler effect. The more subcarriers, the longer the symbol length and the longer guard intervals are possible. DVB-T has two modes: 8k using around 8000 subcarriers and 2k using around 2000 subcarriers. The guard interval parameter determines the signal tolerance to echo. It is always a fraction of the symbol length, thus it takes one of the following values: 1/4, 1/8, 1/16 or 1/32. With the echo problem solved, it is possible to build spectrum-efficient Single Frequency Networks (SFNs). Networks like this are easy to expand using simple repeaters and gap fillers.

As far as the channel bandwidth is concerned, depending on demands, 6, 7 or 8 MHz can be used and the following modulation formats are possible: QPSK (Quadrature Phase Shift Keying), 16-QAM (Quadrature Amplitude Modulation) and 64-QAM.

Depending on the chosen parameters, the DVB-T capacity ranges from 4.98 Mbit/s (4-QAM with guard interval 1/4) to 31.67 Mbit/s (64-QAM with guard interval 1/32). For example, in Finland the 8k mode with 64-QAM and 1/8 guard interval has been chosen, resulting in 22.12 Mbit/s [2].

In DVB-T, MPEG-2 is typically used for compression, although the standard allows usage of other schemes such as H.264/AVC (Advanced Video Coding) as an alternative. MPEG-2 allows multiplexing of separate elementary streams related to the same service (an example here would be an Electronic Service Guide displayed along with the show). Features such as encryption and authorization of end-users are also supported.

3.2.2   Digital Video Broadcasting Handheld

Although the DVB-T transmission system has proved its ability to serve fixed, portable and mobile (like in buses in Singapore) terminals, handhelds have some additional requirements that had to be considered to fully exploit the possibilities. The main problem relates to the power consumption – handheld (meaning battery-powered) devices do not have enough power to receive an ordinary DVB-T signal for a reasonable length of time. The following additional issues needed to be addressed:

- As the devices are battery-powered, the transmission system should offer the possibility of turning off at least a part of the hardware (receiver) to preserve the battery life.

- As it's targeting nomadic users, the system should allow continuous reception of service after leaving a given cell and upon entering a new one (seamless handover).
- As it's expected to serve various scenarios of use (indoor, outdoor, inside a moving vehicle), the system should offer sufficient flexibility to enable access to services at different speeds, locations and conditions.
- As the services are going to be provided in an environment experiencing high noise levels, the transmission system should incorporate means to mitigate these negative effects.
- As it aims to become a worldwide standard, the system should be flexible enough to be used in various transmission bands and channel bandwidths [3].

To address these and other particular requirements, in 2002 the DVB Project started working on the technical standard, originally denoted DVB-X or DVB-M (Mobile), and finally completed as DVB-H (Handheld).

DVB-H builds upon the principles of DVB-T, introducing additional elements in the physical layer and in the link layer. In the link layer these are mainly time slicing and additional Forward Error Correction (FEC) coding. The aim of time slicing is to reduce the average power consumption in the terminal (by 90–95%) and to enable smooth and seamless frequency handover when a user leaves one service area and enters a new cell. Forward Error Correction for Multiprotocol Encapsulated data (MPE-FEC) gives an improvement in the carrier-to-noise (C/N) performance and Doppler performance in mobile channels and, moreover, improves tolerance to impulse interference. While talking about the link layer, it is worth mentioning that the payload of DVB-H is IP datagrams encapsulated by using MPE (Multiprotocol Encapsulation).

In the physical layer there are three main extensions. First, two additional bits were added in the Transmitter Parameter Signaling (TPS) to indicate the presence of DVB-H services and the possible use of MPE-FEC to enhance and speed up service discovery. A cell identifier is also carried in TPS bits to support quicker signal scan and frequency handover. Second, the new 4k mode of Orthogonal Frequency Division Multiplexing (OFDM) was adopted for trading off mobility and the Single Frequency Network (SFN) cell size, allowing single-antenna reception in medium SFNs at very high speeds. This also adds flexibility in network design. Third, an in-depth symbol interleaver for 2k and 4k modes has been defined (interleaves the bits over two or four OFDM symbols, respectively). Thanks to this, the robustness in the mobile environment is improved and also the tolerance to impulse noise is raised to the level achievable with the 8k mode.

Figure 3.4 shows the conceptual structure of a DVB-H receiver. It includes the DVB-H terminal and DVB-H demodulator. The DVB-H demodulator consists further of a DVB-T demodulator, a time-slicing module and an MPE-FEC module. The following actions are involved in the demodulation process:

- DVB-T demodulator recovers the MPEG-2 Transport Stream packets from the received signal. It offers three transmission modes: 2k, 4k and 8k with the corresponding signaling.
- The time-slicing module aims at reducing the receiver power consumption and at the same time enabling smooth and seamless handovers.
- The MPE-FEC module offers additional forward error correction, allowing the receiver to cope with difficult receiving conditions.

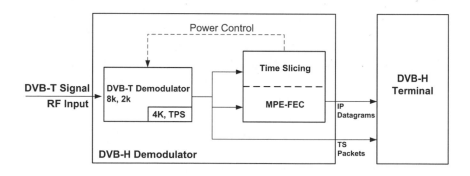

MPE-FEC: Forward Error Correction for Multiprotocol Encapsulation
TPS: Transmitter Parameter Signaling
TS: MPEG-2 Transport Stream
RF: Radio Frequency

Figure 3.4   Structure of a DVB-H receiver [4]

DVB-H transmission can be used for providing IP services along with traditional MPEG-2 services. Figure 3.5 shows the architecture in which MPEG-2 services and IP-based ones share the same multiplexer. The handheld terminal decodes IP services only.

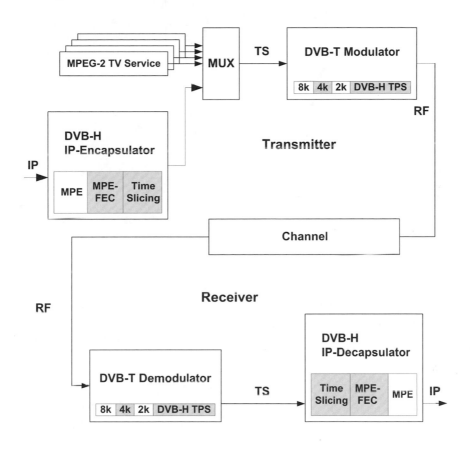

Figure 3.5 A conceptual description of using the DVB-H system (shared multiplexer) [4]

Figure 3.6 presents the possible network topology solutions for DVB-H. On the left-hand side we can see a single rural DVB-H cell and on the right-hand side a DVB-H Single Frequency Network is shown.

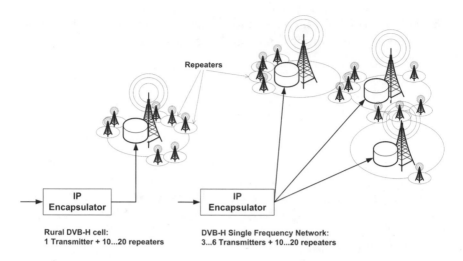

Figure 3.6 Possible network topology solutions for DVB-H [5]

3.2.2.1   Time Slicing

In every handheld device, battery life is of crucial importance. Users prefer to operate for several days without having to recharge. In order to reduce the amount of energy consumed by the devices, DVB-H introduces *time slicing*. Another objective of the idea is to enable smooth and seamless service handover.

In a typical situation, handheld DVB-H devices receive audio/video services transmitted over IP on an Elementary Stream (ES), which has a fairly low bitrate (150 kbit/s to 250 kbit/s) in comparison to the MPEG-2 transport stream (TS) (bitrate of 11 Mbit/s). Therefore, the ES that we are interested in occupies only around 2% of the total MPEG-2 transport stream. It would then be ideal if the receiver analyzed only 2% of the MPEG-2 transport stream that we are interested in. With time slicing this is possible, as the MPE sections of a particular ES are sent in a high bitrate burst. During the time between the bursts, no sections of a particular ES are transmitted, thus the device's receiver can be completely powered off (see Figure 3.7).

The receiver will, however, need to know when to power up again to be ready for receiving the next burst. To inform the receiver when it should expect the next burst, the time (*delta-t*) to the beginning of the next burst is signaled in the header of all sections of the burst. Thanks to this, the receiver can only remain active for a fraction of time, the fraction that is relevant to us.

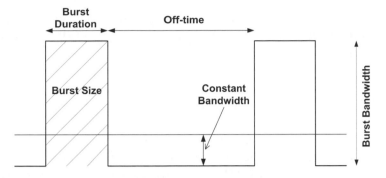

Figure 3.7   Principle of time slicing [6]

Let us make some calculations. If the average bitrate of an ES is 200 kbit/s, the peak bitrate is 10 Mbit/s and the burst size is set to the maximum allowed value of 2 Mbit, then the burst time becomes 200 milliseconds and the burst cycle is 10 seconds. We also have to remember that the receiver has to prepare to receive the sections; the preparation time is estimated to be around 250 milliseconds. Including the preparation time and a slight *delta-t* jitter, the power saving here reaches around 95%. Figure 3.8 shows how power saving depends on the burst bitrate and the bitrate of the ES.

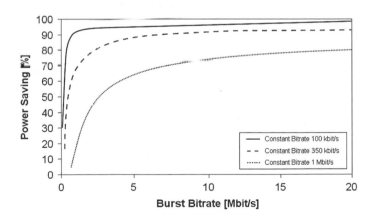

Figure 3.8   Relationship between burst bitrate and power saving [4]

There is also another advantage of time slicing. During the off-times, that is between the bursts, the receiver monitors neighboring cells, scans the frequencies in order to find a potentially better alternative and also executes the actual handover. As the switching of the reception from one transport stream to another occurs during the off period, we are experiencing the optimum handover decision (without interrupting the service reception) as well as seamless service handover.

3.2.2.2 Multiprotocol Encapsulation – Forward Error Correction

The IP datagrams are carried in the MPE section in a standard DVB way, irrespective of whether MPE-FEC is used or not. In the generic case, the use of MPE will add 11–13% overhead. Each section carries, in the section header, the start address for the pay-load. This address indicates the byte position in the application data table (part of the MPE-FEC frame, carrying the application data) of the first byte of the section payload and is signaled in the MPE header. The receiver is then able to put the datagram in the right position in the application data table and mark the positions as 'reliable' for the Reed–Solomon (RS) decoder, provided that the CRC-32 (Cyclic Redundancy Check) indicates that the section is correct.

Because mobile devices have small, usually internal, antennas and require reception from many different directions, there is a need for robust transmission with solid error protection. The objective of MPE-FEC is to improve the carrier-to-noise (C/N) and Doppler effect performance in mobile channels as well as improving tolerance to interference. This goal is achieved by introducing an additional level of error correction to the MPE layer. Along with normal MPE sections carrying data, special, separate MPE-FEC sections are sent, containing parity data calculated from the datagrams. Thanks to this, despite very bad reception conditions, error-free datagrams are obtained after MPE-FEC decoding. However, after applying MPE-FEC, the parity overhead rises to about 25%. Nevertheless, the use of MPE-FEC is optional and can be compensated by applying a slightly weaker transmission code rate.

Now we should take a closer look at how the whole system works. When using MPE-FEC, the IP datagrams of each burst are protected by Reed–Solomon parity data (RS data). The parity data is calcu-lated from the relevant IP datagrams. The RS data is encapsulated in MPE-FEC sections, sent in the same burst, immediately after the last MPE section, in the same elementary stream. The receiver discrim-inates between the two types of sections on the basis of the table_id. In Figure 3.9, we can see the MPE-FEC frame. It consists of the

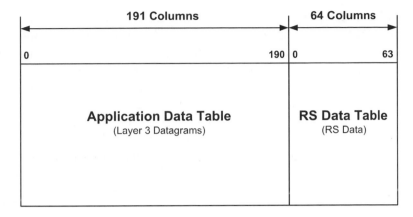

Figure 3.9   Structure of the MPE-FEC frame [7]

Application Data Table (ADT), which hosts the IP datagrams, and the RS table, which hosts the RS data [6].

The last section of the ADT contains the table_boundary flag, indicating the end of IP datagrams in the table. If all previous sections within the ADT were received without any errors, the receiver does not need to receive any MPE-FEC sections; it can just be switched off without receiving and decoding the RS data. This, again, gives some savings on battery consumption, while still providing a thorough error correction mechanism.

3.2.2.3   4k Mode and In-depth Interleavers

The 4k modulation mode was not originally included in the DVB-T standard. It has been introduced in DVB-H in addition to the previously used 2k and 8k modes. The main objective of the 4k mode is to improve network flexibility by trading off mobility and the Single Frequency Network size. The 2k mode is four times more robust to terminal speed than the 8k mode but, unfortunately, Single Frequency Network realization is difficult with this mode due to interference. With the 8k mode, on the other hand, the possible reception speed of the terminal is considerably lower. The 4k mode combines the advantages of the two above, allowing the creation of wide area Single Frequency Networks and also reaching a high terminal speed. In other words, the 4k mode provides wide enough spaces between the subcarriers for fast mobility, while the signal element period is long enough for cells of about 30 km in diameter [2].

Additionally for the 2k and 4k modes, the in-depth interleavers increase the flexibility of the symbol interleaving, allowing the choice of inner interleaver to be independent of the transmission mode used. Thanks to this feature, the 2k or 4k mode signal can benefit from the memory of the 8k signal interleaver to multiply the symbol interleaver depth and thus improve reception in fading channels. Although this approach affects the physical layer, the equipment complexity does not increase significantly over the ordinary DVB-T standard. Figure 3.10 presents elements of the DVB-T system affected by introducing the 4k mode [3].

3.2.2.4 DVB-H Signaling

The DVB-H system should provide robust and easily accessible signaling to the receivers, thanks to which the service discovery is speeded up and enhanced. TPS (Transmitter Parameter Signaling) is used at the multiplex level, thus it is easier and faster to demodulate information carried in TPS than the information in the MPE header. The signaling is used to announce the use of both time slicing and MPE-FEC as well as the 4k mode option.

First of all, the unused combinations of TPS bits have been used to signal new transmission parameters:

- The 4k mode is signaled as an additional transmission mode apart from the basic 2k and 8k modes.
- The DVB-T hierarchy information is used to specify the symbol interleaver depth (e.g., in-depth).
- The cell identifier, optional for standard DVB-T, becomes mandatory for DVB-H (in the case of SFN, there is only one identifier).

Secondly, the two previously unused bits have been allocated exclusively for DVB-H signaling as follows:

- one of the bits indicates the use of time slicing, and
- the second one informs that at least one DVB-H service in the transmission channel is protected by MPE-FEC [4].

It is worth mentioning that the DVB-H signaling is fully backward compatible with DVB-T. It simply employs bits left for future use, which are currently ignored by DVB-T receivers.

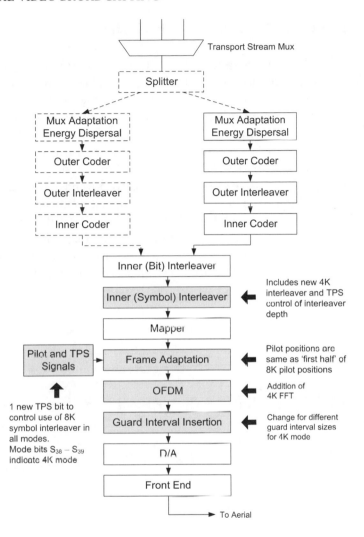

Figure 3.10   Functional block diagram of the DVB-H transmission system (affected blocks shaded) [4]

3.3   ELECTRONIC SERVICE GUIDE

It is essential to understand that it does not matter how great or interesting the provided IPDC service is, if nobody knows about it or if a potential user does not know how to tune the terminal to be able to receive it. An intuitive, reliable and effective way to announce all available services and to describe media had to be developed.

The Electronic Service Guide (ESG) contains information about the digital mobile broadcast services available. Through the information in the ESG a user can select, view and purchase the service or data he/she is interested in. The ESG, in contrast to the ordinary EPG (Electronic Program Guide) used in digital TV, is not restricted to announcing audio/video content, but also proposes other services, such as file downloading, to users. Along with a description of the available content, the ESG provides all the information necessary for the terminal to connect to the related IP stream in the DVB-H transport stream. In Figure 3.11 we can see a Nokia proprietary ESG solution.

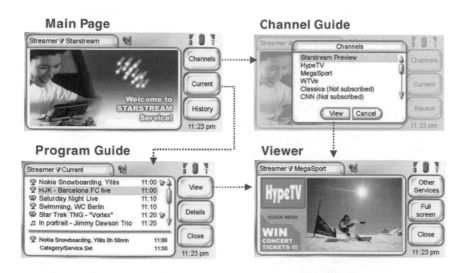

Figure 3.11   Nokia ESG solution (reproduced by permission of © 2008 Nokia Corporation) [8]

After the terminal is activated and has synchronized to a transport stream carrying IPDC data, the ESG starts operating. There is a special dedicated DVB-H time-sliced channel for ESG broadcasts.

We can distinguish the following three main processes within the ESG operation (see Figure 3.12):

- **ESG bootstrap:** the terminal learns which ESGs are available and how to acquire them.
- **ESG acquisition:** the terminal gathers and processes the ESG information either after powering up or after being idle for a long time.
- **ESG update:** the terminal refreshes the stored ESG information, replacing it with the newest versions.

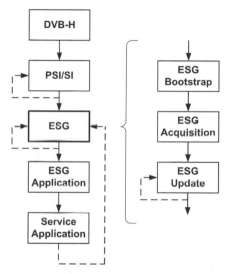

ESG: Electronic Service Guide
PSI/SI: Program Specific Information / Service Information

Figure 3.12   ESG operation diagram [9]

The following ESG layers have been defined:

- **Data model:** defines a set of data structures describing available services (Name, Media title, Description, Genre, Parental rating, Language codes, User rating). The set of ESG data describing available IPDC services is called ESG Instance.
- **Representation:** supports fragmentation of an ESG Instance to ESG XML fragments, thus minimizing the amount of data

delivered to users (allows updating of only certain parts of ESG data).

- **Encapsulation:** ESG fragments are encapsulated into containers, thanks to which ESG information is transmitted in units of a considerable size.
- **Transport:** achieved by using FLUTE (File Delivery over Unidirectional Transport) sessions for optimal delivery of containers as files [9].

Figure 3.13 presents the structure of the ESG. We can distinguish the following three main functional groups: Provisioning, Core and Acquisition. There is also the DCO (Datacast Operator) block, describing the datacast operator, which manages the Service Operation Center (SOC); it also includes the Rights Issuer.

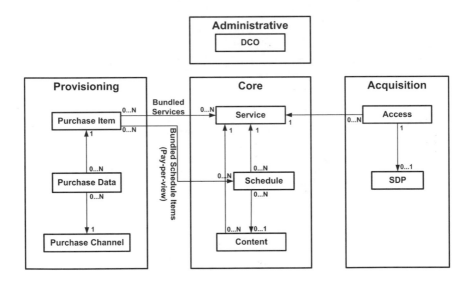

DCO: Datacast Operator
SDP: Session Description Protocol

Figure 3.13 ESG structure [10]

The Core fragments (Service, Schedule and Content) provide information regarding the current service, its contents and about the schedule of the items. They simply carry most of the information displayed to the users. The Service fragment carries data which is static in nature, containing metadata about the digital mobile broadcast service. The Content fragment describes the programming or content which is part of the service. Finally, the Schedule fragment indicates the period of time when the content is available in the broadcast channel.

The Provisioning fragments (Purchase Item, Purchase Data and Purchase Channel) are needed for purchasing of services that are not available without subscription. Thanks to these, a user gets information about their availability and pricing. The Purchase Item fragment bundles some services together so that the user can purchase them as a whole. The Purchase Data fragment indicates a purchase channel from which the service can be purchased, also providing such details as the price. The Purchase Channel represents a system from which access and content rights can be obtained.

Last but not least, the Acquisition fragments include details needed for accessing and consuming the service. Here we get to know how to find the service (Access) and what the service options are, such as language, restrictions (SDP – Session Description Protocol). Moreover, the SDP description contains parameters related to service protection, if it is applied [10].

3.4 STREAMING

IPDC was developed for transmission of any kind of data. However, its main services are based on audio and video streaming. The data transmission rate of 22 Mbit/s is suitable for providing 50 high quality TV channels, which makes this technology very attractive. It establishes a new quality of audio and video transmission in mobile devices. In this section we will describe the details of data streaming in IPDC.

Shaded elements in Figure 3.14 present the protocol stack used in data streaming. This is the basis for our further discussion.

The DVB-H standard is the basis of the IPDC technology. It provides data transmission over a broadcast network using an MPEG-2 transport stream. Regular data, as well as data streams, can be encapsulated into its datagrams using two different techniques. The first one is Multiprotocol Encapsulation (MPE). It is a standardized method based on the MPEG-2 control plane. However, it adds a lot of overhead. For that reason, Ultra Lightweight

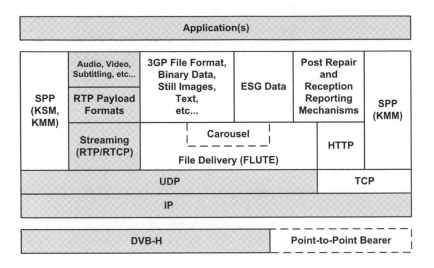

SPP: Service Purchase and Protection
KSM: Key Stream Message
KMM: Key Management Message
ESG: Electronic Service Guide
FLUTE: File Delivery over Unidirectional Transport

Figure 3.14 Basic protocol stack for content delivery (shaded elements responsible for data streaming) [11]

Encapsulation (ULE) was developed. This encapsulates data directly into an MPEG-2 transport stream with a relatively small overhead, which makes it light and easy for processing. These features give it supremacy over MPE [12, 13].

The next two layers are also common for streams and regular data. Internet Protocol and User Datagram Protocol (UDP) are responsible for data transmission at the network and transport layer, respectively. Real-Time Transport Protocol (RTP) and RTP Control Protocol (RTCP) are the first streaming-related elements of the protocol stack [14]. Some specific features are added to RTP/RTCP for implementation in IPDC [11]. For example, the receiver shall not send any RTCP Receiver Reports. Moreover, the sender shall not provide any Reception Reports in its Sender Reports.

Basically, every data type suitable for streaming is possible; however, audio and audio/video streams are most common. In this case, video compression protocol standards, like VC-1, H.264/AVC (Advanced Video Coding) or even H.263, can be used on top of the RTP protocol. One of the profiles of Advanced Audio Coding (AAC) can be used as a compression method in the audio coding.

Figure 3.15 will help us to explain how the signal is processed in the receiver.

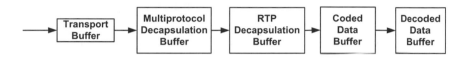

RTP: Real-time Transport Protocol

Figure 3.15 Hypothetical receiver buffering model [11]

The Transport buffer contains an MPEG-2 TS (transport stream). Its main role is to remove duplicate packets (in case any appear). The second module, as might be expected, is responsible for MPE decapsulation. As its output we get IP datagrams. Therefore, at this point we have RTP packets with bursty content wrapped into IP datagrams. The RTP decapsulator removes the RTP payload and handles the time-sliced nature of the content. Thus, a smooth, constant bitrate stream is sent to the Coded Data buffer input. Actions of the last two elements are specified in the media decoder specification.

Streaming over IPDC is about more than just television. Many other video-based services can be implemented. Video transmissions from some events like concerts or sports games are a relevant example. Videoconferences or video-on-demand (VoD) also seem to be useful services when talking about audio/video streaming. However, here we have to deal with a lower scalability and lower bandwidth efficiency/reuse due to individual needs of customers. Also, a good supplement to the mentioned services is audio streaming (digital radio or audio transmission). Thanks to the implementation of an appropriate billing system, users can be charged for those services or these can simply be free.

3.5   DATA TRANSMISSION

The main services of IPDC are based on streaming. However, file delivery is also available and plays an important role in the system. It is a basis for some services supporting streaming such as the ESG or other standalone services. In IPDC, every data item is wrapped into IP packets, thus regular file delivery is not a problem.

Figure 3.16 presents the protocol stack of IPDC. The elements taking part in file delivery are shaded and are discussed later in the section.

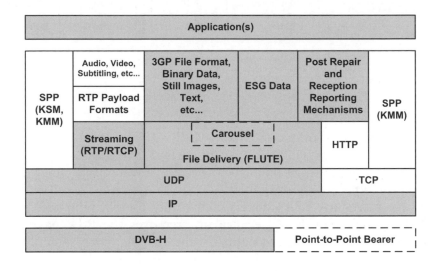

SPP: Service Purchase and Protection
KSM: Key Stream Message
KMM: Key Management Message
ESG: Electronic Service Guide
FLUTE: File Delivery over Unidirectional Transport

Figure 3.16   Basic protocol stack for content delivery (shaded elements responsible for file delivery) [11]

The DVB-H standard, as well as IP and UDP protocols, is responsible for data transmission in general. Thus, all of these are used both in file delivery and in streaming. The MPEG-2 transport stream is used for transmission in the DVB-H standard. The means of data encapsulation is exactly the same as described earlier in Section 3.4.

IP and UDP are also common protocols used in the network and transport layers, respectively.

The most important part of the file delivery system is File Delivery over Unidirectional Transport (FLUTE) [15], and because of that we will describe it in greater detail. Figure 3.17 presents its architecture.

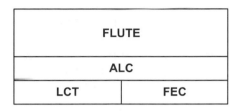

FLUTE: File Delivery over Unidirectional Transport
ALC: Asynchronous Layered Coding
LCT: Layered Coding Transport
FEC: Forward Error Correction

Figure 3.17 Architecture of FLUTE [15]

FLUTE itself is used for the purpose of content description. It uses a File Delivery Table (FDT), which provides the means to describe various attributes associated with the file. The FDT's structure is not fixed. Some properties of the FDT are obligatory and must be a part of the object description. However, a relatively large group of optional properties exists. This makes FDT and FLUTE a very flexible description method.

Objects provided by Asynchronous Layered Coding (ALC) are the bases for FLUTE description [16]. ALC was developed for massive delivery of binary objects over a multicast system. It is very scalable, unidirectional and reliable. It provides the following two main content delivery methods:

- **push service method:** the sender initiates the connection and the receiver joins the channel automatically when appropriate content appears;
- **on-demand method:** the sender multicasts the content continuously for some time and the receiver joins the channel and uses the content when necessary (an example here would be software updates).

ALC is an instance of the Layered Coding Transport (LCT) build-ing block and inherits from it the session concept [17]. The session is a group of logical channels originated by one sender. Moreover, ALC provides a congestion control mechanism and uses Forward Error Correction (FEC).

File delivery over FLUTE complements the main streaming-based services by providing an ESG or subtitles, for example. Moreover, while the system is capable of delivering any binary data, it is pos-sible to implement any data-based services. This opens a vast range of possibilities and the number of potential services is practically unlimited.

3.6   INTERACTION CHANNEL

We have to be aware that the DVB-H broadcast network is uni-directional. Of course, the services can still be provided without any interaction channel, but if one is present, the possibilities are broadened considerably. To provide interactivity, i.e. to allow con-tent selection and ordering/purchasing, a separate uplink interaction channel is a necessity. As the devices we are mainly interested in are mobile phones, all of these requirements can be met with the use of existing cellular networks (Figure 3.18).

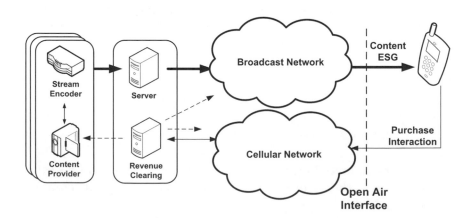

ESG: Electronic Service Guide

Figure 3.18   Implementation of interaction channel [18]

Before we move to describing the advantages of implementing a communication channel, we shall briefly describe the possible channels themselves.

The Global System for Mobile communications (GSM), also denoted here as 2G, was standardized in the early 1990s and, with some improvements, is still the worldwide standard for cellular networks. It was originally designed to support basic voice and data transfer services as well as to enable roaming. GSM is based on TDMA (Time Division Multiple Access), providing very low data rates (up to 9.6 kbit/s for a standard channel). Apart from voice, additional services such as the Short Message Service (SMS), voice mail, call forwarding and displaying the incoming call number were also offered.

Implementation of a packet switch domain in addition to the circuit switched domain led to the creation of an extension to GSM described as 2.5G. The two main improvements are GPRS (General Packet Radio Service) and EDGE (Enhanced Data rates for GSM Evolution). With the use of GPRS, the transmission speeds can reach up to 115 kbit/s and if EDGE is employed, the value rises to 473.6 kbit/s, which enables faster downloads and, therefore, new bandwidth-consuming services can be introduced. There is also one additional feature of packet switched networks called 'always on'. We gain constant access to the medium, paying not for the usage time but only for the amount of data actually transferred. This is just perfectly suited to our needs, such as requesting content or casting a vote in a poll.

Last but not least, there is 3G, defined as a set of mobile technologies using dedicated network equipment, handsets and base stations, all in order to provide high-speed Internet access and data downloads, video services (video call, streaming) as well as ordinary voice calls. In particular, high bitrates were the main requirement for 3G, along with bandwidth on demand, multiplexing of services with different demands and, importantly, inter-system handovers between 3G and 2G networks (coexistence of 2G and 3G networks). Basically, 3G provides speeds up to 2 Mbit/s, but additionally with the use of HSDPA (High Speed Downlink Packet Access), it is theoretically possible to reach 14.4 Mbit/s on the downlink. 3G was supposed to be a single, unified worldwide standard but, unfortunately, the ITU-T (International Telecommunication Union – Telecommunication Standardization Sector) could not reach a consensus among different players, and five different variants have been standardized. The two main ones are known as WCDMA (Wideband Code Division Multiple Access, in Europe denoted UMTS – Universal Mobile Telecommunications System) and CDMA2000. WCDMA, as the name implies, uses Wideband CDMA. As a wider spectrum is used (typically 2×5 MHz), data can be sent and received faster and more effectively. All users share the same carrier and also share the carrier's power. The transmission bandwidth is the same for all data rates. CDMA2000 uses one or more arbitrary 1.25 MHz channels for each direction of communication in the existing 5 MHz spectrum and, more importantly, the already paid frequency spectrum. Its main advantage is that deployment requires only relatively modest hardware and software updates of the existing CDMA infrastructure. 3G can be thought of not only as an interactive channel for broadcast services, but also as an addition in situations where broadcast is not effective. An example would be video-on-demand, transmitted only to one user, where applying the whole broadcast network is not relevant.

Now let us come back to discussing the straightforward advantages of implementing an interaction channel. First of all, cellular networks offer the two-way access necessary for content purchase (Digital Rights Management) and the use of other additional services related to the mobile broadcast service (browsing Internet pages which are a supplement to the service). Also, the local guide services can provide users with information concerning a particular city or region (all thanks to the location information available in cellular networks), such as weather forecasts, programs of the nearby movie theater along with the movie trailers, etc.

Beyond the connection itself, a cellular operator offers much more in the form of sophisticated user authentication (SIM card based), advanced billing services (charging for ordered content) and also has a database of users who might be interested in buying the services. Most importantly for operators, all of the above generate additional revenue streams and enhance the value of the technology to the consumer. From the operators' point of view we can mention:

- increased online traffic on cellular networks (opening pages related to the show watched);
- increased use of premium SMS/MMS (for example, downloading ring tones based on a song of an artist just seen on a music channel);

- increased use of email/MMS (sharing links with friends);
- triggering online sales (buying gadgets with the show's logo, downloading games) [19].

The customer, however, benefits as more and more services and opportunities are offered to him.

To sum it all up, thanks to the convergence of broadcast and cellular networks, the strengths of both technologies are combined, which is beneficial for the user as well as for the operators (Figure 3.19).

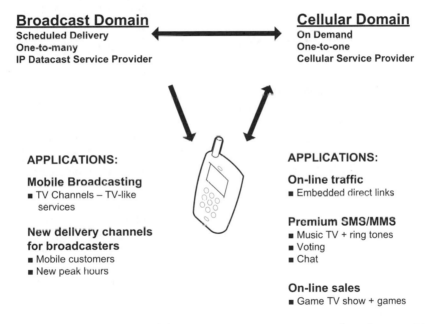

Broadcast Domain
Scheduled Delivery
One-to-many
IP Datacast Service Provider

Cellular Domain
On Demand
One-to-one
Cellular Service Provider

APPLICATIONS:

Mobile Broadcasting
■ TV Channels – TV-like services

New delivery channels for broadcasters
■ Mobile customers
■ New peak hours

APPLICATIONS:

On-line traffic
■ Embedded direct links

Premium SMS/MMS
■ Music TV + ring tones
■ Voting
■ Chat

On-line sales
■ Game TV show + games

Figure 3.19 Broadcast mobile convergence (integrating broadcast with interactive) [20]

REFERENCES

[1] DVB Document A098 (November 2005), *IP Datacast over DVB-H: Architecture,* http://www.dvb-h.org.
[2] L. Staffans, Master's Thesis, *Internet Protocol Datacasting: A Technology Overview,* Helsinki University of Technology,

Telecommunications Software and Multimedia Laboratory, Espoo, Finland, 2004.

[3] ETSI EN 302304 v1.1.1 (2004–11), *Digital Video Broadcasting (DVB); Transmission System for Handheld Terminals (DVB-H)*.

[4] ETSI TR 102377 v1.2.1 (2005–11), *Digital Video Broadcasting (DVB); DVB-H Implementation Guidelines*.

[5] Digital Terrestrial Television Action Group (DigiTAG), *Television on a handheld receiver – broadcasting with DVB-H*, DigiTAG handbook, 2005.

[6] G. Faria, J. A. Henriksson, E. Stare and P. Talmola, 'DVB-H: Digital Broadcast Services to Handheld Devices,' *Proceedings of the IEEE*, 94(1), January 2006.

[7] ETSI EN 301192 v1.4.1 (2004–11), *Digital Video Broadcasting (DVB); DVB specification for data broadcasting*.

[8] NOKIA, *Electronic Service Guide within the Nokia IPDC Solution 2.2*.

[9] DVB Document A099 (November 2005), *IP Datacast over DVB-H: Electronic Service Guide (ESG)*, http://www.dvb-h.org.

[10] NOKIA, *Mobile Broadcast: Open Air Interface 1.0; Service Guide*, August 2005.

[11] DVB Document A101 (December 2005), *IP Datacast over DVB-H: Content Delivery Protocols (CDP)*, http://www.dvb-h.org.

[12] B. Collin-Nocker and G. Fairhurst, *ULE versus MPE as an IP over DVB encapsulation*, http://www.gcs-salzburg.at.

[13] T. C. Hong, W. T. Chee and R. Budiarto, 'Simulation and Design of IP over DVB using Multi-Protocol Encapsulation and Ultra Lightweight Encapsulation,' *National Computer Science Postgraduate Colloquium 2005 [14] (NaCSPC'05)*, Penang, Malaysia, 27–28 June 2005.

[14] RFC 3550 (H. Schulzrinne, S. Casner, R. Frederick and V. Jacobson), *RTP: A Transport Protocol for Real-Time Applications*, July 2003.

[15] RFC 3926 (T. Paila, M. Luby, R. Lehtonen, V. Roca and R. Walsh), *FLUTE – File Delivery over Unidirectional Transport*, October 2004.

[16] RFC 3450 (M. Luby, J. Gemmell, L. Vicisano, L.Rizzo and J. Crowcroft), *Asynchronous Layered Coding (ALC) Protocol Instantiation*, December 2002.

[17] RFC 3451 (M. Luby, J. Gemmell, L. Vicisano, L.Rizzo, M. Handley and J. Crowcroft), *Layered Coding Transport (LCT) Building Block*, December 2002.

[18] A. Ikonen, 'Technology Availability for Mobile Broadcasting,' *Frequency Management for Mobile Broadcasting and IP*

Datacast in Europe – Open Workshop, Copenhagen, 27 September 2005.

[19] NOKIA, *Bringing TV into Mobile Phones*, Forum Nokia's Mobile Application Summit, Singapore, 18 June 2004.

[20] NOKIA (Mobile TV Forum), *Mobile TV Broadcasting*, http://www. nokia.com/ mobiletv, 2005.

4

Multimedia Broadcast/ Multicast Service (MBMS)

One of the aims of today's cellular network operators is to offer appealing multimedia services. However, when many users would like to access the same multimedia service at the same time, even in high-bandwidth networks like UMTS, the available radio resources might just not be sufficient. A remedy to this inefficient resource usage is delivering the content from a single source to a large number of users simultaneously; the data is transferred in parallel, sharing the same resources. The possible benefits were the motivation behind forming study groups within 3GPP (Third Generation Partnership Project), which created and standardized *Multimedia Broadcast and Multicast Service* (MBMS).

MBMS is defined as a unidirectional point-to-multipoint (PTMP) bearer service in which data is transmitted from a single source entity to multiple recipients. It is offered via existing UMTS (Universal Mobile Telecommunications System) cellular networks (with a few enhancements), but is also backward compatible with standard GSM networks (MBMS services provided over both WCDMA-based UTRAN[1] and GSM/EDGE-based GERAN[2]). Generally, it is a solution for transferring audio and light video clips, although real-time streaming is also supported. However, when we are dealing with

---

[1] UMTS Terrestrial Radio Access Network
[2] GSM Edge Radio Access Network

Multimedia Broadcasting and Multicasting in Mobile Networks
G. Iwacz, A. Jajszczyk and M. Zajączkowski
© 2008 John Wiley & Sons, Ltd

heavy duty streaming for wide audiences over a large geographical area, other solutions, such as the already mentioned DVB-H, are more suitable. Thus, MBMS can be treated as a complement to dedicated broadcast networks by delivering local content to a limited audience over smaller coverage areas. This situation may, however, change when High Speed Downlink Packet Access (HSDPA) is commonly implemented. With this enhancement, the MBMS possibilities will be greatly increased, allowing, amongst other things, higher data rates and new services. Furthermore, as MBMS may be regarded as an addition to 3G systems, it may be implemented and launched only in selected cells. This reduces the initial costs, as we focus on selected network areas, and thus may be a good choice at an early stage of development of mobile TV services.

The following sections will present the general system overview and will then focus on the system's detailed architecture, possible services and other relevant aspects. Business aspects and existing implementations will be covered in the following chapters.

4.1 MBMS OVERVIEW

MBMS focuses mainly on the efficient management of core network and radio resources, reusing as much of the existing functionality as possible. Within the network architecture we have only minor changes and one additional component called the BM-SC (Broadcast/Multicast Service Center), which will be discussed in greater detail in Section 4.2. As for the network resources efficiency, MBMS must be deployed in the core network, but also in the UTRAN. The closer the multicast functionality is pushed towards the end-user terminals, the more efficient the system is and the greater are the bandwidth savings.

MBMS has the following two modes of operation:

- broadcast;
- multicast.

The broadcast mode refers to a unidirectional PTMP transmission of multimedia data from a single source to all the users that are found within the defined broadcast service area. All users are generally entitled to receive the service. There is no specific requirement to activate or subscribe to MBMS in the broadcast mode. Consequently, in this mode, charging data will not be generated at the MBMS Transport Service layer. The radio resources (also the core network as multicast is employed) are used efficiently since the data is transmitted over a common radio channel. Transmission of MBMS data adapts to the RAN (Radio Access Network) capabilities and radio resource availability by, for example, reducing the bitrate of data. As not everybody wants to receive the particular service (e.g., receiving the network welcome messages), users can disable reception of the broadcast service on their terminals.

All the mentioned properties also apply to the multicast mode, with the difference that in the multicast mode users have to subscribe to a particular multicast group to be able to receive the service. So the multicast mode is also defined as a unidirectional PTMP transmission of multimedia data from a single source to all users that are found within the defined multicast service area. This mode uses radio resources in an efficient way by transmitting data in a common channel. Here also, the MBMS transmission adapts to the RAN capabilities and radio resource availability. One difference in the multicast mode is that there is a possibility for the network to selectively transmit to cells, within the multicast service area, which contain members of the multicast group.

Moreover, MBMS data can be transmitted either by using point-to-point (dedicated channel) or PTMP (common channel) links. Since WCDMA is an interference-driven radio technology, it is sometimes more efficient to deliver data by using several point-to-point bearers than by a single PTMP bearer. The choice of which of the options should be used for delivering a particular service depends on the number of users in a cell interested in the service. The operator defines a threshold value on which the selection of the bearer is based. An example of a service using the multicast mode would be sports event results transmission, which requires a subscription, for which the subscriber is charged.

In both multicast and broadcast modes the multicast services cannot be guaranteed over the radio network. Nevertheless, the reliable data transmission of applications and services can be secured using proper higher layer methods for protecting data [1].

While talking about the service availability, it is worth mentioning that MBMS supports handovers. A user moving from one cell to another will be able to continue receiving multicast services throughout the multicast service area in which the service is provided.

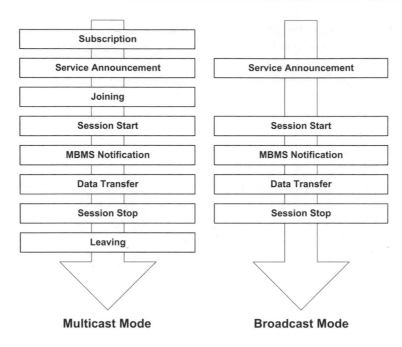

Figure 4.1 Phases of MBMS service provisioning in the multicast and broadcast modes [3]

Figure 4.1 shows the phases of MBMS service provisioning in the multicast and broadcast modes. In the broadcast mode the following stages can be identified:

- **Service Announcement:** during this phase the users are informed about the services currently active or those that will become active at some time, the parameters required for service activation and other required service parameters.
- **Session Start:** a trigger to establish the MBMS bearer for data transfer.
- **MBMS Notification:** to inform the user equipment about the forthcoming/ongoing MBMS data transfer.
- **Data Transfer:** MBMS data is transferred to the user equipment.
- **Session Stop:** at this point the BM-SC determines that there will be no more data to send for some period of time and the bearer resources are released [2].

If the data is transmitted in the multicast mode, the following three additional phases are required:

- **Subscription:** this is the agreement of a user to receive services offered by a specific service provider; subscription information is recorded in the appropriate database in the operator's network.
- **Joining:** once a service has been announced, a subscriber can join a multicast group; a user indicates his/her interest to receive a service.
- **Leaving:** a user indicates interest to stop service data reception; MBMS deactivation occurs.

As we said earlier, MBMS multicast must be deployed in the core network but also in the UTRAN. For the core network, several approaches can be taken into consideration, such as IP multicast. In UTRAN, the situation is more complicated. The data is transmitted using a common bearer, thus each of the multicast group members might expect very different signal conditions. Since all signals in UMTS are sharing the same bandwidth and overlapping in time, it is essential to introduce control to maintain an acceptable Signal-to-Interference Ratio (SIR) for all users. In order to obtain this, power control is used, which employs feedback requests from the terminals concerning the bandwidth. Thanks to this, each Node-B transmits using the minimum power needed for maintaining the required SIR ratio, thus diminishing power consumption. The point-to-multipoint power control mechanism will be similar to that for point-to-point, but for MBMS channels a grouped decision has to be made, thus a nonoptimal decision might be made for some nodes [4].

Another issue is that, just as with DVB-H, service announcement is of crucial importance; users will not use the service if they do not know about it. That is why an easy to access and simple Electronic Service Guide is necessary. It informs users about the services both in the multicast and broadcast modes, additionally allowing downloading teasers (an advertisement that gives a little information about a product to make the customers curious to learn more), previews, etc. The announced services can also be correlated with location information (a user receives information related to his/her current location).

4.2 MBMS ARCHITECTURE

As we stated earlier, the essential role of MBMS is data delivery from one sender to multiple recipients. Concerning the architecture,

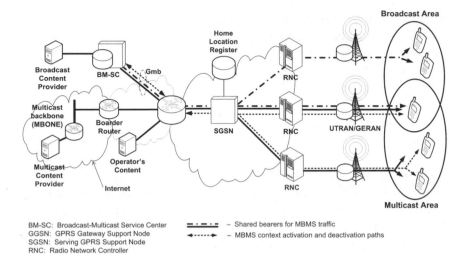

Figure 4.2   Logical MBMS architecture designed by 3GPP [5]

MBMS is realized by adding a few extra components to the ordinary 3GPP network and by widening the functionality of the existing components. The MBMS architecture proposed by 3GPP is presented in Figure 4.2. The most significant architecture components are described in the following passages.

MBMS can run over UTRAN as well as over GERAN. This means that MBMS can be used in 2G, 2.5G and 3G mobile networks. UTRAN/GERAN is responsible for efficient data delivery in the MBMS service area. Moreover, it must support mobility of MBMS receivers, which can, however, lead to a limited data loss. That is why the MBMS services should be able to cope with potential data loss caused by the users' mobility. Additionally, UTRAN/GERAN is able to transmit service announcements and other services in parallel to MBMS. Also, the radio bearer can be chosen according to the number of users within a cell.

The SGSN (Serving GPRS Support Node) is responsible for data routing between an operator's nodes, for session control and management. It also takes care of users' mobility and is responsible for switching data traffic between GSM and UMTS networks. Apart from this, in MBMS it has some additional functions. The SGSN performs user individual MBMS service control and supports mobility procedures. It gathers all users of the same MBMS service into a single MBMS service area. Furthermore, it maintains a single connection with the MBMS service provider and provides the transmission to the UTRAN/GERAN. The SGSN is also involved in charging procedures. It generates charging data per multicast MBMS bearer service. It does not perform charging itself, though.

Generally, the GGSN (GPRS Gateway Support Node) provides the connection between a mobile network and other networks, like the Internet. Here, it is connected to the BM-SC module and is a termination for MBMS GTP (GPRS Tunneling Protocol) tunnels. It links these tunnels via IP multicast with the MBMS data source. The GGSN is also responsible for the bearer plane for broadcast and multicast MBMS transmission. On the other hand, it can provide features supporting the MBMS bearer service such as, for example, charging data collection.

The BM-SC (Broadcast/Multicast Service Center) plays the role of an MBMS data source. As it is the most important part of the MBMS architecture, its internal structure and functionality will be discussed in greater detail.

The BM-SC provides functions for MBMS service provisioning and delivery, including (Figure 4.3):

- Membership function;
- Session and Transmission function;
- Proxy and Transport function;
- Service Announcement function;
- Security function.

The Membership function is responsible for user authorization. It can provide access to the service for an authorized user or deny it for an unauthorized one. Therefore, it may have access to the user data needed for authorization. It also may generate charging records.

The Session and Transmission function is much more complex. Its essential role is to send MBMS data. Therefore, it is able to schedule MBMS session transmissions and retransmissions. Moreover, it marks the retransmission sessions to allow the user equipment to distinguish between different ones. The transmission and retransmission or retransmissions of a certain session have a common identifier. This identifier has two or three octets and it is passed by the application layer in the content. Additionally, the Session and Transmission function provides appropriate transport-associated parameters to the GGSN. These can be, for example, quality parameters or

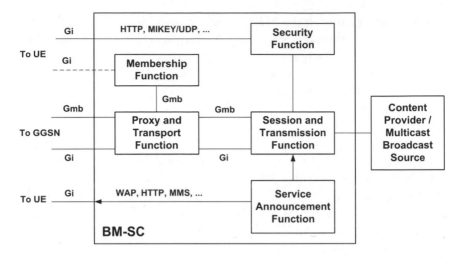

UE: User Equipment
GGSN: GPRS Gateway Support Node

Figure 4.3   BM-SC functional structure [3]

service area information. Furthermore, this function authorizes and authenticates the external data sources and accepts content from these.

The Proxy and Transport function plays the role of a proxy agent for signaling between GGSNs and other BM-SC subfunctions. Routing of the different signaling interactions is transparent to the GGSN. The Proxy and Transport function also generates charging records for the content provider. We can divide this function into the following subfunctions:

- Proxy function managing the control plane;
- Transport function managing the multicast payload.

The Service Announcement function is a user service level function. It provides information about MBMS broadcast and multicast services. It announces the general service information to the user equipment. This can consist of video and audio encodings, for example. Moreover, session description information should be announced. All announcements should use IETF specified protocols over the broadcast and multicast MBMS bearer service. The service announcement is triggered by the BM-SC; however, it does not have to be sent from the BM-SC. The service announcement should support the following mechanisms [3]:

- MBMS bearer capabilities to advertise MBMS user services;
- Push mechanisms (WAP push);
- URL (Uniform Resource Locator) through WAP, HTTP;
- SMS (point-to-point);
- SMS-CB (cell broadcast).

Last but not least, there is the MBMS Security function [6]. This is essential when the multicast mode is discussed. To deliver data in this mode, an appropriate security system is necessary to prevent unauthorized access. It is extremely important when we consider charged services. The security system consists of the user authentication, key distribution and data protection methods. The main issue in multicast security is key distribution when the key has to be delivered to a group of users instead of a single entity. Thus, the MBMS Security function's basic role is MBMS key distribution. All other tasks can be performed using point-to-point solutions, utilizing the point-to-point security protocol called AKA (Authentication and Key Agreement) [7]. The key itself should change in time in order to ensure service reception by new users and to prevent users who have left the service from accessing it.

Apart from the functional entities, Figure 4.2 presents many reference points. However, we will focus only on Gmb, as this is the most significant. At this point, signaling between the GGSN and the BM-SC is exchanged. This includes user-specific signaling responsible for [3]:

- the BM-SC authorization of user service activation at the GGSN;
- GGSN reports about users' successful service activation;
- GGSN reports about service deactivation or release.

It also includes MBMS bearer service signaling related to:

- establishment and registration of MBMS Bearer Context to the BM-SC by the GGSN;
- MBMS Bearer Context release by the GGSN or BM-SC;
- session start and stop indication to the GGSN by the BM-SC.

Moreover, the BM-SC uses the Gmb to initiate the deactivation of the MBMS bearer service when the MBMS user service is terminated. Additionally, different network elements can provide user-specific and MBMS bearer service signaling. Further, BM-SC functions may be provided by other physical network elements. Thus, the Gmb protocol must provide GGSN transparency.

To complete the architecture description, two relevant concepts will be introduced. The first one is the MBMS UE Context, which contains user equipment information (such as MBMS bearer service related information) and is created when a user joins the particular MBMS bearer service. UE, SGSN, GGSN and BM-SC membership functions are involved in MBMS UE Context creation. Moreover, the SGSN creates extra information related to user equipment mobility.

The second concept is the MBMS Bearer Context. It is created in the SGSN or GGSN while the first MBMS UE Context is created or when a downstream node requests it. It contains full information about a particular MBMS bearer service and is statically configured in the BM-SC Proxy and Transport function. The MBMS Bearer Context can be in one of two states: 'Active', when a particular service is running and the session is active, or 'Standby', when the session is inactive and no bearer plane resources are required.

Another issue worth considering is the Quality of Service (QoS). All parameters related to QoS in UMTS can be found in [8]. They are also used in MBMS; however, the following limitations exist [3]:

- only Background and Streaming classes are supported;
- only higher SDU (Service Data Unit) error ratio is supported;
- the guaranteed bitrate of a streaming traffic class depends on radio resource usage by other services;
- maximum bitrates differ.

The Streaming class is important to MBMS, as many significant services are streaming based. The packet transfer delay should be minimized and packet dropping should be used for traffic flow adjustments.

The Background class, on the other hand, is used for low bitrate services, like messaging or file downloads. This class does not impose as strict delay and packet loss requirements as the Streaming class. Background class traffic can be shaped and packets can be dropped to adapt to the currently available resources. Further, in case of unsatisfying transmission parameters, the service can switch to the

Streaming class to provide reliable data transmission. The Streaming class guarantees appropriate bitrate, while the Background class data is transmitted without any guaranteed data bitrate. Thus, in order to provide reliable data delivery in case of a high data loss, a retransmission mechanism is incorporated in the Background class.

4.3 MBMS SERVICES

Generally, MBMS does not provide any content services itself, but a wide set of applications can use its bearer capabilities to create new services. Thus, MBMS can be regarded as an enabler of other services. Any kind of service is applicable, regardless of the content, as long as the limitations of the data transmission (data rate, etc.) do not cause major problems to the quality of service. Although MBMS provides relatively high data rates, making it possible to deliver more and more multimedia, bandwidth-demanding services, it might not be an optimal solution for providing long-duration broadcasting streams like television programs. As we said before, this kind of service can be handled more efficiently by DVB-H networks. Of course, delivering, for example, television channels over MBMS is possible, but the technology is better suited to complementing broadcast networks.

There are the following three main types of MBMS User Services [9]:

- **Streaming service:** a continuous data flow providing a stream of continuous media, like audio and video, is a basic MBMS User Service. Also, supplementary information of text and/or still images is delivered along with an audio/video stream. For example, if text includes URLs of some content on the Internet, a user can easily access the content without entering the URL manually.
- **File download service:** this service basically delivers binary data over an MBMS bearer. An MBMS-enabled user terminal activates an appropriate application and utilizes the delivered data. The most important functionality for this service is reliability; a user must receive all the sent data in the proper order to experience the service.
- **Carousel service:** this is a service that combines aspects of both the streaming and file download services described above. Similar

to the streaming service, this one also includes time synchroniz-ation. However, the target of this service is only static media. It is a method for delivering content by repeating or updating the transmission of the data cyclically.

In addition to the above-mentioned division, many others can be drawn depending on:

- whether the broadcast or multicast mode is used;
- what media types are transmitted via this broadcast or multicast service;
- what the charging characteristics are.

Table 4.1 presents some of the typical MBMS services, divided into four groups as proposed in [10].

Table 4.1   Typical MBMS services [10]

Live events (video/audio)	Sports ('live goal'), news clips, music events, financial updates, traffic info, weather info, audio event channels, electronic classroom (E-learning, document push)
Area targeted	Weather info, local advertising, alert/emergency, shopping channel, local news, city entertainment (e.g., events, restaurants), expo services, airport/train station channel, local events
Profile/preference based	Subscription news, stock quotes, webcasting, corporate push
e-Commerce	Shopping channels, teletext-type services, marketing info push

A couple of the mentioned services as well as their extensions are briefly discussed below:

- **News clips:** the content should be differentiated to separate different news channels: main news, sports results, economics, etc.
- **Localized services:** this could be, for example, a tourist inform-ation channel, showing the most important places to visit, recommending restaurants, etc.
- **Combined audio and video clip services:** here, the scope of applic-ation is very wide; we can mention advertisements, interactive television voting and real-time betting.
- **General content distribution:** downloading files (possible to use FLUTE), HTTP, video, audio; can be also used for software updates.

- **Announcement services:** announcement services to a wide audience, either in the broadcast (to all users) or in the multicast (to a certain group) mode. These can include commercial or electronic tickets, and can also serve as a marketing tool.
- **Multipoint-to-multipoint services:** videoconferencing, multiplayer games, multiparty messaging.

The user is able to manipulate the content delivered over MBMS, including forwarding it by using, for example, MMS or Bluetooth. It is also possible to store the content in a user terminal and access it at a later time. However, care must be taken to fulfill requirements concerning Digital Rights Management. This issue is solved by applying an appropriate DRM system. A selection of existing DRM systems is described in Chapter 6.

The supported media types are independent of the specific data types and formats. At a minimum, the following media types are supported by MBMS:

- text (embedded hyperlinks and additional text presented along with, for example, video);
- still images;
- video;
- speech;
- mono/stereo audio.

The MBMS User Service supports standardized mechanisms of transferring charging-related information. The following charging mechanisms are supported:

- charging on a subscription basis (a user buys a subscription for the appropriate service in advance and is granted access to the service for a period of time; during the lifetime of a subscription to a multicast service, it is possible for the user to declare service preferences);
- charging for keys that allow the user access to the data (a user chooses a particular content and purchases the keys necessary to access it).

The subscription or key purchasing mechanism is provided thanks to the use of the uplink channel, already described earlier in Section 3.6. All the steps necessary to protect the content, distribute the access keys or to charge for the content are carried out by the BM-SC module (described earlier in Section 4.2).

4.4 PERFORMANCE OF MBMS

In the previous sections we have learned a lot about MBMS. To summarize a little, MBMS is a multicast technology enhancing the capabilities of existing 3G (also 2.5G) networks. It brings us resource savings since the same content is delivered to a group of terminals. Moreover, it may be treated as a software upgrade and thus can be implemented in selected cells only. On the terminal side, only a minor software upgrade is needed to accommodate this multicast technology. In conclusion, MBMS is relatively cheap and fast to implement. The question is why is it not the preferred technology? Why do operators invest money in dedicated systems such as DVB-H instead of implementing MBMS? The answer becomes clear when we compare the performance of these competing technologies.

MBMS, when implemented over a WCDMA network consuming 5 MHz bandwidth, allows for data rates of approximately 2.5 Mbit/s. With DVB-H networks, the data rates depend on several parameters. Assuming 8 MHz bandwidth, the available transfer rates

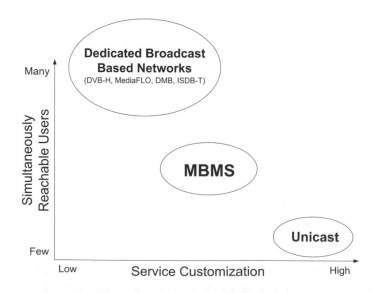

Figure 4.4 Comparison of MBMS with other media delivery approaches [11]

start from 5 Mbit/s. By an appropriate selection of transmission para-meters, the value can be increased to up to 31 Mbit/s. Of course, changing some of the parameters in order to increase the data rates may cause degradation of other transmission performance indicators such as reception quality or coverage. Nevertheless, the advantages of dedicated multicast technologies are significant.

Despite the relatively low transmission speed, MBMS is still a very promising technology. In our opinion, it will become an ulti-mate solution in many 3G networks all over the world. The main aim is to limit the resource usage when relatively light content is considered. Figure 4.4 presents a comparison of MBMS and other content delivery techniques.

REFERENCES

[1] 3GPP TS 22.146 v8.0.0 (2006–06), *3rd Generation Partnership Project; Technical Specification Group Services and System Aspects; Multimedia Broadcast/Multicast Service; Stage 1 (Release 8).*

[2] C. Herrero and P. Vuorimaa, *Delivery of Digital Television to Handheld Devices*, Helsinki University of Technology, Espoo, Finland.

[3] 3GPP TS 23.246 v6.10.0 (2006-06), *3rd Generation Partnership Project; Technical Specification Group Services and System Aspects; Multimedia Broadcast/Multicast Service (MBMS) Architecture and functional description (Release 6).*

[4] P. Eusébio, A. Marquet, N. Martins and A. Correia, 'Management Scenarios for Multicast Groups in Enhanced-UMTS,' IEEE 60th *Vehicular Technology Conference*, Los Angeles, California, USA, 26–29 September 2004.

[5] 3GPP TS 23.846 v6.1.0 (2002-12), *3rd Generation Partnership Project; Technical Specification Group Services and System Aspects; Multimedia Broadcast/Multicast Service (MBMS) Architecture and functional description (Release 6).*

[6] 3GPP TS 33.246 v0.1.0 (2003-04), *3rd Generation Partnership Project; Technical Specification Group Services and System Aspects; Security; Security of Multimedia Broadcast/Multicast Service (Release 6).*

[7] 3GPP TS 33.102 v4.4.0 (2002-06), *3rd Generation Partnership Project; Technical Specification Group Services and System Aspects; 3G Security; Security Architecture (Release 4).*

[8]   3GPP TS 23.107 v4.4.0 (2002-03), *3rd Generation Partnership Project; Technical Specification Group Services and System Aspects; QoS Concept and Architecture (Release 4)*.

[9]   3GPP TS 22.246 v8.0.0 (2006-06), *3rd Generation Partnership Project; Technical Specification Group Services and System Aspects; Multimedia Broadcast/Multicast Service (MBMS) use services; Stage 1 (Release 8)*.

[10] Alcatel (Strategy Whitepaper), 'Multimedia Broadcast and Multicast Services in 3G Mobile Networks,' *Alcatel Telecommunications Review* – 4th Quarter 2003/1st Quarter 2004.

[11] P. Nordlöf, *3G TV*, Ericsson, 2006.

5

Alternative Technologies

Apart from the two previously described technologies: DVB-H-based Internet Protocol Datacasting and Multimedia Broadcast/Multicast Service, several other technologies have been developed and are either at a commercial or trial stage around the world. These are, in particular: MediaFLO, Digital Multimedia Broadcasting (both S-DMB, a satellite-based technology, and T-DMB, a terrestrial-based technology) and Terrestrial Integrated Services Digital Broadcasting (ISDB-T). Currently, the above-mentioned technology standards are competing to emerge as the dominant technology standard in mobile broadcast television. In the following sections we shall provide further insight into each of these technologies. Finally, in the last section of this chapter, a comparison of all these technologies, covering their main features as well as similarities and differences, will be presented.

5.1 MEDIAFLO

MediaFLO is a multicast system based on the FLO (Forward Link Only) technology. Both were developed in the USA by Qualcomm Inc. FLO uses a dedicated Single Frequency Network (SFN) utilizing Orthogonal Frequency Division Multiplexing (OFDM). The system can operate at various frequencies and bandwidths, providing audio/video streaming services along with IP-based data downloads. The offered services are accessible with the help of an easy-to-use program guide user interface. FLO is, to some extent, similar to

Multimedia Broadcasting and Multicasting in Mobile Networks
G. Iwacz, A. Jajszczyk and M. Zajączkowski
© 2008 John Wiley & Sons, Ltd

DVB-H and it is the most promising alternative among the broadcast technologies. The most significant difference between these competing solutions is the fact that FLO is a closed standard. Before we discuss why this matters and how it influences the technology itself, we are going to provide some general information about the architecture, performance and various technical aspects of FLO.

5.1.1 Architecture

FLO stands for Forward Link Only. However, it is obvious that an uplink is also necessary and this is a part of the FLO architecture. The system obviously requires radio transmitters and MediaFLO capable terminals. What is interesting is that content providers are not part of the system; still, they are an important part of the service chain. The most significant element is the Network Operations Center, consisting of the National Operations Center (NOC) and Local Operations Centers (LOCs) [1]. Figure 5.1 shows the FLO architecture.

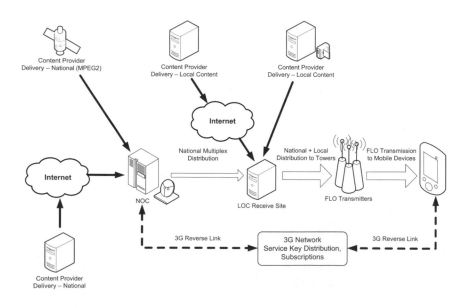

Figure 5.1   FLO technology architecture with external content providers [1]

The most significant and complex system fragment is the Network Operations Center. It is responsible for distribution and content management and may also contain a billing system. Moreover, the Network Operations Center communicates with external operators in matters concerning users' subscriptions as well as the delivery of access and encryption keys. It also provides billing information for these networks. On one hand, it is a gateway for content providers and on the other, it provides a ready service to the network of transmitters. The Network Operations Center is divided into two separate parts: nationwide (NOC) and local (LOC). It may include one or more LOCs to serve as an access point from which local content providers can distribute local content to mobile devices in the associated market area.

Next, we have the transmitters. The FLO air interface is designed to support frequency bandwidths of 5, 6, 7 and 8 MHz and the transmitter can operate at a wide range of frequencies. Moving on to terminals, due to power-saving mechanisms, these devices can operate for a relatively long time, providing high quality services. Then, there is the reverse channel. Its role is to provide user-generated information back to the FLO infrastructure. Key distribution and subscriptions are two examples of the information types transmitted via uplink. Finally, we have the content providers. As we mentioned before, content is out of the FLO's scope. However, it is worth mentioning that there may be various sources of content, including the Internet or satellite signals.

5.1.2 System Performance

According to the FLO technology review [1], it can deliver up to 15 high quality (30 frames per second, QVGA) video streams with stereo audio containing wide-area content and five local market specific streams. To achieve this, H.264 coding is used. If a non real-time transmission is considered, MediaFLO can provide up to 50 nationwide and 15 local channels, each providing up to 20 minutes of content per day. This improvement is possible with the use of background media delivery, as the submitted service can be uploaded to the terminal during idle times. This approach forces the content to be available before transmission. Additionally, not only video streams can be transmitted; IP data is acceptable as well. This allows the delivery of information like weather forecasts, stock market ratings, etc.

One of the interesting features of the FLO technology is the mechanism called *layered modulation*. The transmission is divided into two layers:

- **Base layer:** this provides 15 frames per second video pictures and has extended coverage.
- **Enhanced layer:** this is available in addition to the base layer when the signal-to-noise ratio (SNR) is high enough. In practice, it is available almost everywhere and provides 30 frames per second video streaming.

When considering mobile devices such as terminals, power consumption becomes the key issue. FLO provides a mechanism that can extend a device's operation time by significantly reducing the power consumption. Similarly to DVB-H, FLO's air interface uses Time Division Multiplexing (TDM). Since the stream is sent with some intervals, the signal receiving circuits can be shut down during the idle times to save battery power. This downtime depends on the stream itself, as the content size and transmission rate are issues here. Also, the behavior of different frequencies differs and some fade faster than others. Thus, FLO uses frequency diversity to provide better reception in various conditions. Using both the mentioned mechanisms allows provision of the desired QoS. Moreover, signal reception is possible even in difficult usage conditions such as traveling at high velocities. Even at 200 kilometers per hour the reception is of a good quality. Beyond that speed, the quality of service degrades smoothly.

5.1.3 Technical Description

First, let us take a look at FLO's air interface in relation to the OSI/ISO model (see Figure 5.2). FLO's air interface operates at the two lowest layers: physical and data link. The difference when compared to OSI/ISO is that the data link layer in the FLO technology is divided into the Medium Access Control (MAC) layer and the Stream layer.

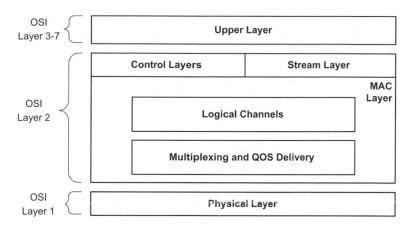

Figure 5.2 FLO's air interface in relation to the OSI/ISO model [1]

Each of the presented layers has its specific role:

- **Upper layer:** this is responsible for control information formatting, content compressing and provisioning and for access control. To provide the needed flexibility to accommodate various services, the FLO's air interface does not enforce the specifics of the upper layers.
- **Stream layer:** this multiplexes up to three flows from the upper layer into one logical channel. It is also responsible for wrapping streams into packets and for error handling functions.
- **Medium Access Control layer:** this controls physical layer access, maps and multiplexes logical channels to physical channels. Moreover, it enforces QoS.
- **Physical layer:** this defines frequencies, modulation and encoding requirements. It also determines the channel structure for the forward link.

Next, we shall focus on the frame structure and the protocol stack. As shown in Figure 5.3, the transmitted signal consists of so-called super-frames. It starts with TDM pilots enabling fast access to OIS (Overhead Information Symbols), which define the placement of content in the super-frame. The content itself is located in four frames (this can be local as well as global content).

The coding rates, as well as the modulation or quality requirements, may differ in different logical channels. The FLO multiplexing

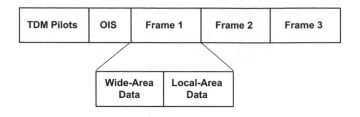

TDM Pilots
OIS
Frame 1
Frame 2
Frame 3
Wide-Area Data
Local-Area Data
TDM: Time Division Multiplexing
OIS: Overhead Information Symbols

Figure 5.3 FLO super-frame structure [1]

scheme allows the user's terminal to decode only a single channel. This feature minimizes the power consumption of the receiver. Still, more than one stream can be decoded – several related channels can be received simultaneously to provide a single high quality service. An example here would be video streaming with a separate audio path.

As we are aware, the less protocol overlay the better, since heavy protocols mean more bits to send. As a result of this, longer transmission is required, which increases the power consumption. In order to overcome this problem, a lot of effort was put into reducing the protocol stack (see Figure 5.4).

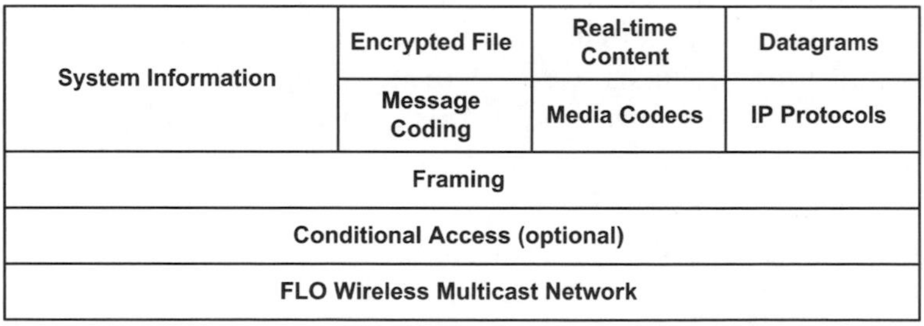

System Information
Encrypted File
Real-time Content
Datagrams
Message Coding
Media Codecs
IP Protocols
Framing
Conditional Access (optional)
FLO Wireless Multicast Network

Figure 5.4 FLO transport protocol stack [1]

The reliability issues also need to be considered. FLO employs a turbo inner code, appropriate when the used bandwidth matters (e.g., in deep-space satellite communication). As an outer code, the Reed–Solomon block-based error correcting code is used. This code is commonly applied in the transmission of digital signals and data storage. Both the mentioned codes provide reliability of data independently. Moreover, both layers are secured independently.

Last but not least, we shall discuss the issue of frequency range. Multicast suitable frequencies do not differ much from those used for unicast IP and voice services. The frequencies span the range between 450 MHz and 3 GHz. As each of us is used to holding the terminal in a position that enables an easy and comfortable view of the device's screen, some frequencies are preferable. Most suitable for this scenario are the 800 and 1900 MHz frequencies. As these are already occupied by the cellular networks, transmission at the frequency of 700 MHz became most desirable. Still, FLO is not bundled to this particular frequency, as many others are supported as well. When bandwidth is considered, FLO can operate at the 5, 6, 7 or 8 MHz band. The available data rates range from 0.47 up to 1.87 bit/s per Hertz. This means that the 6 MHz bandwidth can provide a transmission speed of 11.2 Mbit/s. FLO, just like DVB-H, uses OFDM and supports 16-QAM, QPSK and layered modulation techniques.

5.1.4 Summary

FLO and DVB-H may look similar, and actually are in many technical aspects. However, there is still one essential difference between these two technologies. DVB-H was developed as an open standard by the DVB community, in contrast to FLO, which is a closed, in-house developed standard, the property of Qualcomm Inc. While DVB-H is a technology based on industry consensus, fitting many and various players, FLO is independent. This results in several differences ranging from technical aspects to business issues. When we compare these two, it may seem that FLO's performance is better. This is delusive though. Because of its openness, DVB-H was tested all over the world in various conditions and usage scenarios. Its performance has been proven by a large number of real tests. FLO, on the other hand, as a closed standard has undergone a relatively small number of tests and some data about its performance may be based more on theoretical knowledge than real tests. This leads us to the next significant difference. DVB-H was developed by a community. Thus, it is supported by this community comprising many large, global players. Moreover, the openness means that various companies can join the battle for revenue – a new market opened for many companies as equipment vendors. This causes the technology's fast evolution and spread. Behind FLO we have only a single, although powerful, company, Qualcomm, which is not only developing the

FLO's core, but also producing chipsets, acquiring spectrum, building its own broadcast network, etc. Qualcomm keeps the technology closed and isolated. Thus, in contrast to DVB-H, FLO does not have the advantage of economies of scale. Without this, even a significantly better solution with a better performance will probably not achieve commercial and economic success. There are a lot of different opinions about these two approaches. Time will tell if better performance results will win the battle over the DVB community support.

5.2   DIGITAL MULTIMEDIA BROADCASTING (DMB)

By Digital Multimedia Broadcasting (DMB) we understand a digital transmission system for sending multimedia (data, radio and TV) to different kinds of mobile devices including mobile phones. The technology was developed in South Korea under the national IT project. Although trials were carried out much earlier, the world's first official DMB broadcast was not available until 2005. DMB was derived from the Digital Audio Broadcasting (DAB) standard for radio broadcasting, which was originally developed in the 1980s as a research project in the European Union (Eureka project number EU147) and then in the 1990s rolled out in Canada, most European Union countries and parts of Asia. In the meantime, DAB has been adopted as a European standard by ETSI (European Telecommunications Standards Institute) [2], which, since 2005, has also been responsible for the standardization of DMB [3]. DAB itself provides CD-quality audio streaming but also allows for additional data services. Basically, DMB utilizes the DAB transmission technology. Still, in order to make it operate effectively, it comes with extensions including additional coding schemes for video and audiovisual content. As mobile television programs were to be received by some users traveling at high velocities, the system had to be enhanced with efficient error correction mechanisms. The appeal of the DMB technology is that it is possible to roll it out using current DAB broadcast stations and frequencies, although this results in a limited number of video channels.

There are some similarities between DMB and the main competing mobile TV standard, DVB-H. It can operate via satellite or terrestrial transmission; accordingly, there is a variety of DMB versions, including S-DMB (utilizes a satellite network) and T-DMB (utilizes a terrestrial network). DMB (like DAB) uses frequency channels of 1.536 MHz bandwidth and net data rates between 1 and 1.5 Mbit/s. DMB may operate in different frequency ranges between 30 MHz and 3 GHz. Accordingly, a different transmission mode of DMB is used in a different frequency range. More information on the available modes will be provided in the following sections.

There are several frequency bands which may be used for transmission. T-DMB uses the L band (1452–1492 MHz) and S-DMB uses the S band (2605–2655 MHz). This is accompanied by frequency bands common to both T-DMB and S-DMB. These are in the ranges of 174–240 MHz (band III) [4].

If the allocated frequency range is sufficient, DMB channels can be realized in parallel. When a frequency range of 7 or 8 MHz (bandwidth of a former analog television channel) is used, four channels for the simultaneous transmission of 15 to 20 mobile TV programs can be accommodated.

T-DMB utilizes a network of several transmitters, which may form either a Single Frequency Network (SFN) or Multi Frequency Network (MFN). In DMB, most SFNs occupy frequency channels in band III. The coverage range of a single transmitter may be up to 100 km. When we consider MFNs, the coverage range of a single transmitter is not larger than 25 km. This apparently makes MFNs more expensive than SFNs when we consider the money spent to build a network covering a certain area. Additionally, the complexity, and thus the cost, is even higher, as in the case of MFNs handovers are required. This mechanism has to be implemented at the receiver side so that the reception is not interrupted when moving from one coverage area to another.

When it comes to S-DMB, the transmission range is significantly larger when compared to T-DMB transmitters. An S-DMB satellite placed in a geostationary orbit may cover an area of several hundred kilometers in diameter.

While trials for deployments using DMB have been announced in Europe (including Germany for the World Cup in 2006), South Korea has been the primary supporter of the technology. SK Telecom began offering commercial S-DMB services in May 2005, while T-DMB became available in Korea in December 2005.

One of the strongest aspects of the DMB standard is the possibility to deliver other services apart from video (see Figure 5.5). Still, as video is our primary interest we will start by briefly describing these additional services and then focus only on the video service.

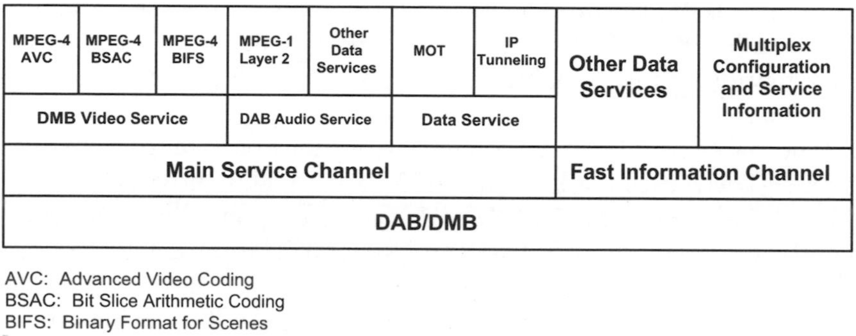

MPEG-4 AVC	MPEG-4 BSAC	MPEG-4 BIFS	MPEG-1 Layer 2	Other Data Services	MOT	IP Tunneling	Other Data Services	Multiplex Configuration and Service Information
DMB Video Service			DAB Audio Service		Data Service		
Main Service Channel							Fast Information Channel		
DAB/DMB									

AVC: Advanced Video Coding
BSAC: Bit Slice Arithmetic Coding
BIFS: Binary Format for Scenes

Figure 5.5   DMB services [5]

The data service is used mainly for two applications, as presented in Figure 5.5, namely IP tunneling and MOT. MOT stands for Multimedia Object Transfer and is a transport protocol used for transmission of multimedia content. In the most common scenario, MOT is used for transmission of frequently demanded data. These can be some web pages or a blockbuster movie accessed via the video-on-demand service. If the payload is too big, as it is with large video transfer, the object is fragmented into smaller segments transmitted in the carousel manner (the transmission is periodically repeated) [6].

Moving on, we have the IP tunneling which enables the use of IP as a common network layer protocol for DAB data services. In the DAB system, the IP datagrams which are to be sent are encapsulated into the MSC (Main Service Channel) data groups. In particular, one datagram is carried in one MSC data group. With the use of the IP tunneling mechanism, all different content types available on the Internet may be accessed via the DMB network. Just as with MOT, thanks to IP tunneling even large files may be transmitted easily to the end-user (e.g., video clips). Also, audio and video streaming is possible [7].

It should be mentioned that the described data services are transmitted without relation to the program. Thus, in contrast to audio and video services, they are referred to as non-program-associated data (NPAD).

As we have already said, DMB is an extension of the DAB standard, which was developed in order to transmit CD-quality audio streams. When we then move to DMB, this functionality is still present as part of the standard. For the audio service the source coding scheme is MPEG-1 Layer 2 and the data rates vary from 8 to 384 kbit/s. What is interesting is that the audio service also allows for transmission of data other than the audio stream. This is called program-associated data (PAD). Of course, in this case we are not talking about transfer of heavy files as we were with IP tunneling or MOT. Often the program-associated data is in the form of a short message presented on the device's display.

Last but certainly not least, there is the video service. This is of particular interest to us as it enables transmission of television programs to mobile devices. However, before the video stream may be passed on to the transmitter itself, it has to undergo three processes presented in Figure 5.6. As can be seen, at first the source coding needs to be applied to the three types of data constituting the video stream (video, audio and interactive content). After that, synchronization occurs and the different data streams are merged in the MPEG-2 multiplexer block. Below we shall discuss the source coding process in more detail.

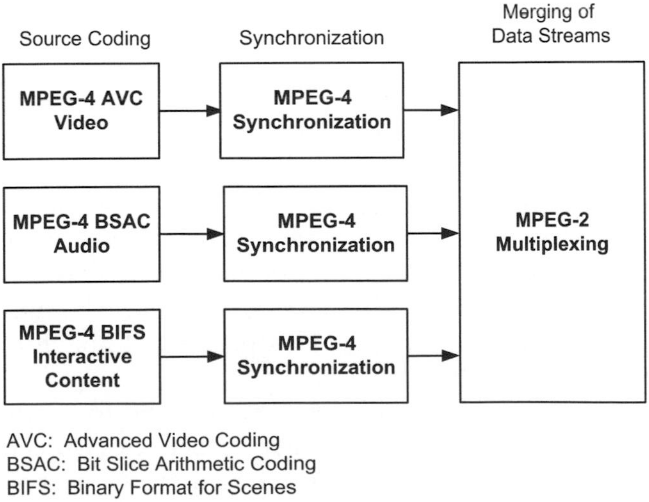

Source Coding	Synchronization	Merging of Data Streams
MPEG-4 AVC Video	MPEG-4 Synchronization	
MPEG-4 BSAC Audio	MPEG-4 Synchronization	MPEG-2 Multiplexing
MPEG-4 BIFS Interactive Content	MPEG-4 Synchronization	

AVC: Advanced Video Coding
BSAC: Bit Slice Arithmetic Coding
BIFS: Binary Format for Scenes

Figure 5.6 Video service multiplexing schema

The aim of source coding is to reduce the amount of transmitted data. This is necessary as the data rate of the DMB channel is limited and has to be utilized effectively (at maximum it is 1.5 Mbit/s). The simplest way to do this is to remove all the redundant information. Such a process may be regarded as compression and employs different techniques for different data types of the video stream. The video streams are compressed by the use of MPEG-4 AVC (Advanced Video Coding) (also denoted H.264 in the ITU terminology), developed by the Moving Picture Experts Group (MPEG) and the International Telecommunication Union (ITU). And, for encoding of audio streams, DMB utilizes MPEG-4 BSAC (Bit Sliced Arithmetic Coding) and AAC (Advanced Audio Coding). Finally, there is the interactive content, which is encoded using the technology called MPEG-4 BIFS (Binary Format for Scenes). The technology allows for sending different parts of the scene (such as musical instruments for a rock concert) separately. Thanks to this, each of the separated objects can be used as an interactive link. In our example, a user could click on a given musical instrument, which has a certain link attached. As a result, a web page of a music shop where the instrument can be purchased may open.

While discussing the source coding, we should be aware that apart from the coding efficiency, we also need to take into account the complexity of the code. After all, the data stream is to be decoded by a mobile terminal having limited resources in terms of available random access memory and CPU power.

5.2.1 Multiplexing and Channel Coding

Before the different data streams of different services may be transmitted, these need to be adapted to comply with certain characteristics of the DAB/DMB channel. This process is called *channel coding*. Following this, different services must be multiplexed into a common transport stream. This process, although a little bit simplified, is presented in Figure 5.7.

As the transmission is prone to errors, in order to secure its reliability and sustain a required Quality of Service (QoS) level, the mentioned channel coding is applied. Based on the original source coded streams, some redundant data is calculated and transmitted alongside. This process actually increases the amount of data to be

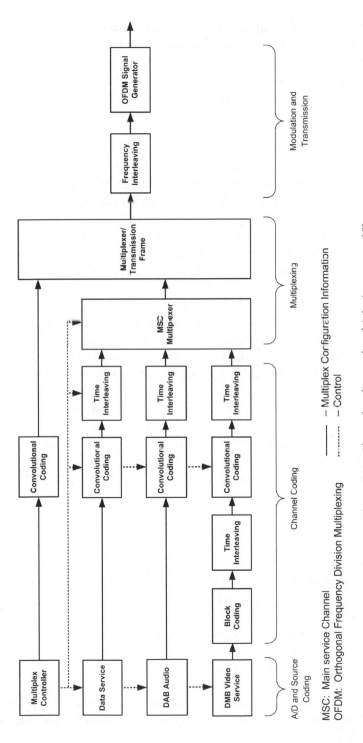

Figure 5.7 Channel coding and multiplexing process [5]

MSC: Main service Channel
OFDM: Orthogonal Frequency Division Multiplexing

———— – Multiplex Configuration Information
·········· – Control

transmitted; however, thanks to this, a given number of transmission errors may be detected and corrected at the receiver side. The described process is presented in Figure 5.7 as the convolutional coding block present for every service type. In the convolutional coding, x bits from a continuous input data stream are taken and then mapped into y bits of the output stream ($y > x$). Thanks to such a process, correction of errors at the receiver side is possible with the use of a Viterbi decoder.

Unfortunately, this approach does not allow us to correct error bursts. To overcome this limitation, a time interleaving process is performed on the output of the convolutional coder. The idea is to divide the data stream into fixed-length words. The bits of one code word are exchanged with the bits of other code words. The process is then reversed at the receiver. This process, however, generates an additional delay, which may not be acceptable for certain types of data like control information. The solution is to send it in the Fast Information Channel (FIC), for which no interleaving is applied.

When considering the video service, one may notice that another stage called block coding or outer coding is present within the process before convolutional coding. The aim here is to enable reception of the signal at high velocities (e.g., 200 km/h) while still maintaining a good quality level.

As presented in Figure 5.7, after channel coding the time-interleaved data streams from several services are multiplexed into a common transport stream. The whole multiplexing process, coordinated by a multiplex controller, is shown in Figure 5.8. The DMB transmission frame contains three fields carrying data for the following:

- **Synchronization Channel:** the information transferred secures synchronization with the receiver by marking the beginning of a frame.
- **Fast Information Channel (FIC):** carries the Multiplex Configuration Information (MCI), which defines the configuration of the multiplex.
- **Main Service Channel (MSC):** carries the data from different DMB services. The MSC is divided into a set of subchannels carrying a single data stream of a particular service.

Here it is worth mentioning one important feature of the DMB system. We are all aware that when a mobile TV service is considered,

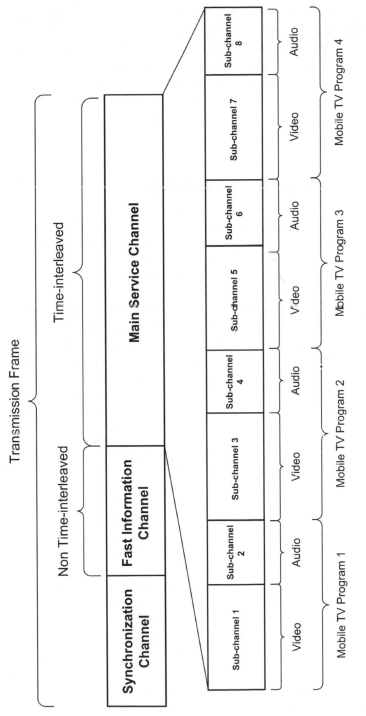

Figure 5.8 DMB transmission frame structure [5]

special attention should be paid to the issue of power consumption. The DMB system offers the possibility for a given receiver to receive and decode the data streams that belong only to the service used. Consequently, when other subchannels are transmitted, the receiver can power off, extending the battery lifespan. This is possible as the receiver is informed by the MCI about the position of a given subchannel within the transmission stream.

5.2.2 Modulation and Transmission

After the multiplexing process the transport stream is broadcast to the receiver over the radio channel. Occupying the bandwidth of 1.536 MHz, the possible data rates are between 1 and 1.5 Mbit/s. The rate depends on the parameters of the convolutional code employed.

When we consider a Single Frequency Network, the coverage of a single transmitter may be up to 100 km in diameter. Unfortunately, as the distance increases, the signal becomes more susceptible to interference. Also, multipath propagation becomes a significant problem. This creates a need for a technique which addresses these issues. DMB systems apply a technique known as multicarrier modulation, where a channel is divided into subcarriers. A single subcarrier is able to transfer data independently of the others.

Unfortunately, the use of multicarrier modulation creates another problem, as it may suffer from side lobes. They do not carry any relevant information but still can distort the transmission in neighboring subcarriers. To overcome these problems, Orthogonal Frequency Division Multiplexing (OFDM) is applied, which has already been tackled in Chapter 3. Here we will only mention that in OFDM, subcarriers are placed orthogonal to each other, solving the described problem.

There are four transmission modes defined for DMB. The aim was to allow the system to be used for different frequency ranges and network configurations. The differences between the modes include symbol duration, guard interval, carrier spacing and the number of carriers in a radio channel of 1.536 MHz bandwidth. Which of the modes should be used is dependent on the system operating conditions (e.g., allocated frequency band). Table 5.1 collates the different parameters of the four transmission modes.

Table 5.1   Parameters of the transmission modes in DMB [2]

	Mode I	Mode II	Mode III	Mode IV
Network	SFN	MFN	Cable or satellite	Terrestrial or satellite
Frequency range	174–216 MHz	1452–1467 MHz	< 3 GHz	T: 1452–1467 MHz S: 1467–1492 MHz
Range	96 km	24 km	12 km	48 km
No. of subcarriers	1536	384	192	768
Space between subcarriers	1 kHz	4 kHz	8 kHz	2 kHz
Symbol duration	1 ms	250 μs	125 μs	500 μs
Guard time	246 μs	62 μs	31 μs	123 μs
No. of bits/OFDM symbol	3072	768	384	1536
Frame duration	96 ms	24 ms	24 ms	48 ms

Mode I is intended for terrestrial Single Frequency Networks and local-area broadcasting in Bands I, II and III. Modes II and IV are preferred for terrestrial local broadcasting in Bands I, II, III, IV and V as well as in the 1452 MHz to 1492 MHz frequency band. This mode can also be used for satellite or hybrid satellite–terrestrial transmission in the L band. Transmission mode III is intended to be used for terrestrial, satellite and hybrid satellite–terrestrial broadcasting below 3000 MHz. Additionally, mode III is preferred for cable distribution (it can be used at any frequency available on cable) [2]. Generally, modes with a high number of subcarriers and long symbol duration should be considered for long-range transmitters. However, when a small delay is a crucial requirement, as it is with satellite broadcasting, modes with fewer subcarriers and shorter symbol duration are appropriate.

After the transmission frames are generated by the multiplexing process, modulation onto the subcarriers of the OFDM radio channel occurs. DMB uses a variant of the Differential Quadrature Phase Shift Keying (DQPSK) modulation schema. The principle of this modulation schema is as follows [5]:

- We take four basic symbols ('00', '01', '11' and '10') and assign each of these a different phase shift: 0°, 90°, 180° and –90°.
- When the next symbol is to be transmitted, the phase of each subcarrier is changed depending on the phase shift determined by the transmitted symbol. The phase shift is dependent on the phase of the previous symbol.

5.2.3 Summary

DMB extends the possibilities offered by DAB and also allows encoding of mobile TV programs. These may then be transmitted to different kinds of mobile devices, including PDAs or mobile phones – generally to any device equipped with a DMB receiver. The system, of course, retains the possibility to broadcast radio channels as defined by DAB. Moreover, delivery of other types of data, including IP-based datagrams, is supported.

5.3 TERRESTRIAL INTEGRATED SERVICES DIGITAL BROADCASTING (ISDB-T)

By Integrated Services Digital Broadcasting (ISDB), we denote a group of digital broadcasting standards in Japan. These cover terrestrial, satellite and cable transmission and all employ a common format for multiplexing. Today, ISDB is used in Japan to provide, amongst other things, a digital service to TV sets and handheld mobile units.

Work on ISDB started in the 1980s at NHK Science and Technical Research Laboratories (STRL) in Japan. At that time the aim was to develop a new digital broadcasting system that could easily accommodate new services, such as high quality audio–video and data broadcasting. The new system was to be based on the following concepts [8]:

- The information broadcast should be converted into digital signals in an integrated manner for processing.
- Different types of transmission media should be supported (e.g., satellite, terrestrial and cable TV networks).
- The services should be available everywhere at any given time, regardless of the transmission medium.

Currently the ISDB standard is maintained by the Japanese organization called ARIB (Association of Radio Industries and Businesses). The MPEG-2 system is used as the digital signal multiplexing scheme and, following this, the MPEG-2 Video/Audio standard is used for audio/video coding.

Table 5.2 presents the different ARIB standards for digital broadcasting. These are ISDB-S (for satellite television), ISDB-T (for terrestrial television), ISDB-C (for cable television) and 2.6 GHz band mobile broadcasting. All of these are based on MPEG-2 video and audio coding as well as the transport stream described by the MPEG-2 standard. ISDB-T and ISDB-T$_{SB}$ (for sound broadcasting) are for mobile reception in TV bands. Additionally, there is the 1seg, an ISDB-T service for reception on cell phones, laptop computers and vehicles. In this section we are going to focus on ISDB-T, as this is employed for delivery of television to mobile devices.

Table 5.2 ARIB standards for digital broadcasting [8]

	Digital Television		Digital Sound	
System	ISDB-S/Wide-band CS	ISDB-T	ISDB-T$_{SB}$	2.6 GHz satellite
Transmission	STD-B20	STD-B31	STD-B29	STD-B41
Source coding and multiplex	Coding and multiplexing STD-B32			
	Service information STD-B10			
Data broadcasting	Presentation engine (BML) STD-B24			
	Execution engine (GEM-based) STD-B23			
Home server	System based on home services STD-B38			
CAS	Conditional access STD-B25			
Receiver	STD-B21		STD-B30	STD-B42
Operational guideline	TR-B15	TR-B14	TR-B13	TR-B26

5.3.1 Overview of ISDB-T

ISDB-T (Terrestrial Integrated Services Digital Broadcasting) is a standard derived from ISDB that is responsible for terrestrial transmission. In 2003 it was adopted for commercial transmission in Japan. A few years later it comprises a market of over 100 million television sets. The characteristics of the ISDB-T system are as follows:

- MPEG-2 Transport Stream is used for multiplexing of digital audio and video to synchronize the output.

- When different digital contents are transmitted simultaneously in a single stream, each can employ a different modulation scheme and appropriate bitrate.
- In order to inform the receiver about a certain multiplexing and modulation configuration, a control signal is added.
- Reception of selected services is possible with a lightweight narrowband receiver, which is called partial reception.

ISDB-T can operate within the 6 MHz bandwidth usually reserved for TV transmission. In such a configuration, two or three SDTV channels can be transmitted. These SDTV channels can also be multiplexed to a single HDTV channel. Moreover, ISDB-T provides interactive services with data broadcasting, including the EPG (Electronic Program Guides). In addition, Internet access is supported as a return channel. It is also claimed that ISDB-T allows HDTV to be received in moving vehicles at over 100 km/h.

ISDB-T can be received indoors with a simple indoor antenna and also outdoors using mobile devices. It provides SFN (Single Frequency Network) and on-channel repeater technology. With SFN we gain robustness to multipath interference and we can efficiently manage the owned spectrum. Also, robustness to electromagnetic interference (e.g., from power lines) is provided, which is important in densely populated areas.

5.3.2 ISDB-T Transmission System

Figure 5.9 presents a diagram of the ISDB-T transmitter. From the input signals of MPEG-2 transport streams, at the output we obtain an IF (Intermediate Frequency) signal. The transmission system includes blocks responsible for remultiplexing, channel coding, modulation and transmission control, which are going to be briefly described in the following sections.

At the beginning of the process the transport stream is remultiplexed and arranged into data groups (data segments). After channel coding, OFDM (Orthogonal Frequency Division Multiplexing) framing occurs. Each of the OFDM segments has a bandwidth of Bo/14 MHz (Bo = 6, 7 or 8 MHz). Thanks to the hierarchical transmission in the channel, the system can adapt to different reception conditions. It is possible to choose transmission parameters independently for each hierarchical layer. Table 5.3 outlines the ISDB-T

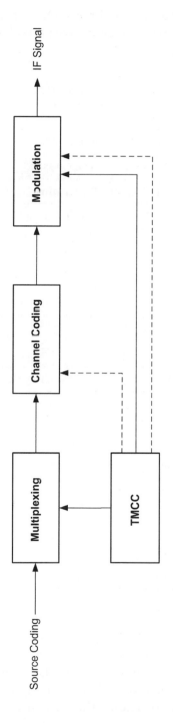

Figure 5.9 Diagram of ISDB-T transmitter [9]

IF: Intermediate Frequency
TMCC: Transmission and Multiplexing Configuration Control

— — Signal Flow
- - - - - — Control Signal

transmission schema and in Table 5.4 three ISDB-T transmission modes with different OFDM carrier spacing have been classified (for a 6 MHz system) [9].

Table 5.3   ISDB-T transmission schema [10]

Item		Contents
Video coding		MPEG-2 Video (ISO/IEC 13818-2)
Audio coding		MPEG-2 AAC (ISO/IEC 13818-7)
Data broadcasting		BML(XHTML), ECMA Script
Multiplex		MPEG-2 systems (ISO/IEC 13818-1)
Conditional access		Multi 2
Transmission		ISDB-T transmission
Channel bandwidth		6 MHz, 7 MHz, 8 MHz
Modulation		Segmented OFDM (13 segment/channel)
Mode, Guard		Mode: 1, 2, 3 Guard interval ratio: 1/4, 1/8, 1/16, 1/32
Carrier modulation		QPSK, 16-QAM, 64-QAM, DQPSK
Error correction	Inner	Convolutional code (Coding rate: 1/2, 2/3, 3/4, 5/6, 7/8)
	Outer	(204, 188) Reed–Solomon code
Interleave		Frequency and time Interleave Time interleave: 0–0.5 s
Information bitrate (depends on parameters)		6 MHz: 3.7–23.2 Mbit/s 7 MHz: 4.3–27.1 Mbit/s 8 MHz: 4.9–31 Mbit/s
Receiver		ISDB-T receiver
Operational guideline		ISDB-T broadcasting operation

As indicated previously, the ISDB-T system offers so-called hierarchical transmission. The idea here is to change the transmission parameters of the modulation scheme for each data segment. The changes may include different lengths of interleaving time or coding rates and are independent of each other. At any one time, a

Table 5.4 ISDB-T transmission modes [10]

	Mode I	Mode II	Mode III
Bandwidth	5.6 MHz (13 segments)		
Carrier spacing	3.968 kHz	1.984 kHz	0.992 kHz
Total number of carriers	1405	2809	5617
Number of symbols per frame	204		
Useful symbol duration	252 µs	504 µs	1.008 ms
Guard interval duration	1/4, 1/8, 1/16, 1/32 of useful symbol duration		
Carrier modulation	QPSK, 16-QAM, 64-QAM, DQPSK		
Inner code	Convolutional code (1/2, 2/3, 3/4, 5/6, 7/8)		
Outer code	RS (204, 188)		
Interleaving	Frequency and time interleaving (2-dimensional)		
Length of time interleaving	0, 0.13, 0.2, 0.5 s		
Information rate	3.65 Mbit/s – 23.23 Mbit/s		

maximum of three layers can be transmitted in a single channel, meaning there can be three OFDM segment groups with different parameters. In ISDB-T systems, multiplexing is performed as defined in the MPEG-2 standard and this also applies to hierarchical transmission.

Another important feature is the possible partial reception. Using a narrowband receiver, one can receive only part of the services contained in a transmission channel. A selected segment in the transmitted signal can be separated and received independently from the others. This is done by limiting the range of frequency interleaving within a segment.

An example of hierarchical transmission and partial reception is presented in Figure 5.10. What can be seen in the figure is that partial reception uses a dedicated central segment of the existing OFDM segments.

In Figure 5.11 we can see the channel coding block, which receives the packet arranged in the multiplex frame and forwards the channel-coded packets to the OFDM modulation block.

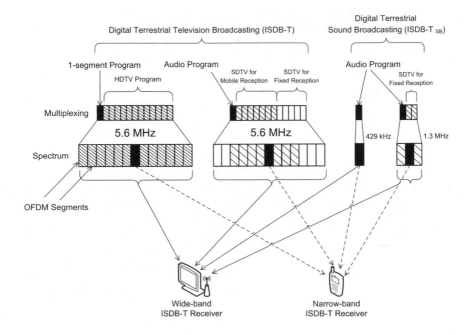

Figure 5.10 Example of hierarchical transmission and partial reception (6 MHz system with 13 segments) [10]

Figure 5.12 shows the OFDM modulation block. This block receives channel-coded transport stream packets from the inner coder. As an outcome we receive the OFDM signal.

When we consider the bit interleaving process from Figure 5.12 it should be remembered that it also causes some delay. The important issue is that the delay differs from stream to stream when different layers are considered. This is because the streams have different properties like channel coding. Of course, this delay needs to be compensated. That is why, in the transmitter, prior to the byte-wise interleaving, a delay adjustment is carried out.

Apart from the bit interleaving, frequency interleaving also occurs. This consists of inter-segment frequency interleaving and intra-segment frequency interleaving. The first is carried out among differential modulation (DQPSK) segments and among coherent

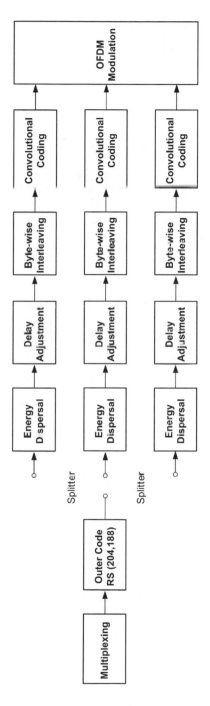

Figure 5.11 Channel coding diagram [5]

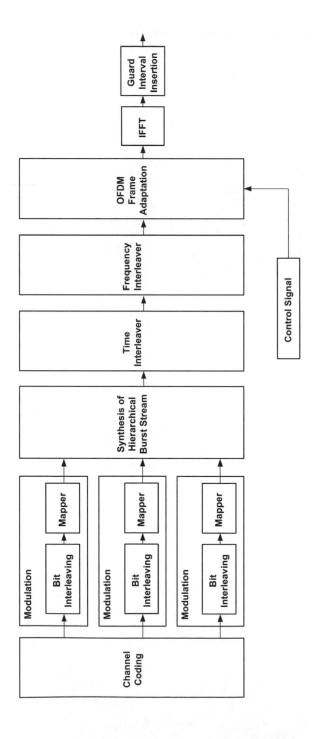

IFFT: Inverse Fast Fourier transformation

Figure 5.12 Block diagram of OFDM modulation [9]

modulation (QPSK, 16-QAM, and 64-QAM) segments. As for the second, a random interleaver may be applied.

Going back to Figure 5.9, another remaining block, labelled TMCC, can be seen. The abbreviation stands for Transmission and Multiplexing Configuration Control. TMCC is a pilot present in every OFDM segment. The information it carries refers to layer configuration of the hierarchical transmission. Moreover, the pilot conveys information not only about the current configuration but also about the next one.

5.3.3 Summary

As a summary we shall list the crucial features of ISDB-T. First of all, the system offers the possibility of broadcasting multiple programs as well as HDTV. This is accompanied by a set of multimedia services (regional information service, quizzes, voting and questionnaires). Secondly, the network can be organized as a Single Frequency Network, which increases the effectiveness of spectrum usage. Moreover, with the system we get a common transmission scheme for both television and sound broadcasting. Extremely importantly, ISDB-T allows mobile reception with receivers even on the move. It is also interoperable with other similar standards such as ISDB-S or ISDB-C. Finally, it should be mentioned that the system enables partial reception with handheld receivers.

5.4 COMPARISON OF TECHNOLOGIES

We believe that DVB-H and MediaFLO are the leading broadcast contenders, while DMB and ISDB-T appear to be regional solutions. Accompanying this, there is, of course, MBMS, which, in contrast to the aforementioned technologies, is not designed for broadcast networks. This technology standard allows operators to use the existing spectrum and cellular networks in order to offer mobile TV and multimedia services to their subscribers. Thus, it should not be considered in terms of a competitor to the broadcast/multicast technologies, but rather as a complementary standard. Table 5.5 gathers together some basic information about each multimedia delivery technology described in this book.

Table 5.5 Comparison of multimedia delivery technologies

	DVB-H	MediaFLO	DMB	ISDB-T	MBMS
Origin	Derivative from DVB-T (Europe), open standard	QualComm packet data technology (USA)	Derivative from DAB (South Korea)	Maintained by ARIB (Japan)	3GPP
SFN	Yes	Yes	Yes [1]	Yes	No
Frequencies	170–230 MHz, 470–862 MHz	450 MHz–3 GHz	30 MHz–3 GHz	UHF (328.6 MHz–2.9 GHz)	UMTS
Most desirable frequencies	< 700 MHz	700 MHz	T-DMB: 1452–1492 MHz S-DMB: 2605–2655 MHz Common: 174–240 MHz	around 900 MHz	UMTS
Frequencies	6, 7, 8 MHz	5, 6, 7, 8 MHz	1.536 MHz	5.6, 6, 7, 8 MHz	N/A
Bitrates	4.98–31.68 Mbit/s per 8 MHz [2]	0.4–1.87 Mbit/s per 1 MHz	1–1.5 Mbit/s	3.7–23.2 Mbit/s(for 6 MHz)	UMTS
Uplink	No	No	No	No	Yes
Frequency or code domain power reduction	No	Yes	Yes	No	No
Time domain power reduction	Yes	Yes	Yes	No	No
Average channel switching time	1.5 s	1.5 s	1.5 s	N/A	
Per channel QoS	No	Yes	Yes	No	N/A
Channels per MHz [3]	1.5	>3	>1.8 [4]	>2.3(for 5.6 MHz)	N/A
Required spectrum for 20 channels	12 MHz	6 MHz	< 11 MHz [4]	˜8.6 MHz	
Commercial availability	Yes	No	Yes (2005)	Yes (2003)	No
Video coding	H.264	H.264	H.264	H.264	H.264
Audio coding	AAC	AAC	AAC+ or AAC-HE	AAC	AAC

1: Possible multi-frequency network in T-DMB
2: Depends on parameters
3: Live channels
4: 15-20/7 or 8 MHz of former analog TV channel

REFERENCES

[1] MediaFLO, *FLO Technology Overview*, Qualcomm Incorporated, 2007.

[2] ETSI EN 300401, *Radio Broadcasting Systems; Digital Audio Broadcasting (DAB) to mobile, portable and fixed receivers*, V1.4.1 January 2006.

[3] ETSI TS 102428, *Digital Audio Broadcasting (DAB); DMB video service; User Application specification*, V1.1.1 June 2005.

[4] ETSI TS 102427, *Digital Audio Broadcasting (DAB); Data Broadcasting – MPEG-2 TS streaming*, V1.1.1 July 2005.

[5] Samsung Telecommunication Europe Whitepaper, *DMB – Digital Multimedia Broadcasting*.

[6] ETSI EN 301234, *Digital Audio Broadcasting (DAB); Multimedia Object Transfer (MOT) protocol*, V2.1.1 June 2006.

[7] ETSI ES 201735, *Digital Audio Broadcasting (DAB); Internet Protocol (IP) datagram tunneling*, V1.1.1 September 2000.

[8] H. Asami and M. Sasaki, 'Outline of ISDB Systems,' *Proceedings of the IEEE*, **94**(1), January 2006.

[9] ARIB (Association of Radio Industries and Businesses) Standard, *Terrestrial Integrated Services Digital Broadcasting (ISDB-T), Specification of channel coding, framing structure and modulation*, 28 September 1998.

[10] K. Yokohata, *ISDB-T: Single transmission for fixed, vehicular and handheld receivers*, NHK (Japan Broadcasting Corporation), Science and Technical Research Laboratories, March 2007.

6

Digital Rights Management (DRM)

As DVB-H is a broadcast technology, everybody within the range of the transmitters can receive the signal and thus access the offered services. This leads to an obvious need to protect the content from unauthorized access. Furthermore, if the content is already down-loaded to an end device, using either DVB-H (IPDC) or a cellular network (MBMS), we need to protect it from further distribution, copying or reselling. In other words, we need a system ensuring that only paying customers are eligible to receive the services as well as accessing the content on their terminals.

After all, operators are eager to invest in the technology only when foreseeing possible profits; offering any kind of service free of charge is not an option. Therefore, the operators run a kind of a 'virtual' shop, selling subscriptions for the basic service package (usually monthly subscriptions) and also specific rights to some additional protected content. All the purchases are recorded in a database, closely correlated with the customer database, and then fed into the billing system to adequately charge the users. What is more, thanks to the gathered information concerning the usage of a particular content or service, the operator can easily share the revenue with the relevant content or service provider.

On the other hand, once the content is downloaded, its use and further distribution has to be controlled in respect of the intellectual property rights. We should be able to specify whether the content can be freely copied to other devices, how many times it can be viewed and many other details concerning access to an already purchased item.

The requirements mentioned above are typically addressed by implementing one of the existing Digital Rights Management (DRM) technologies. Below, some of the available protection schemes shall be presented, focusing mainly on those used in already existing implementations.

6.1   OMA DRM V2.0

OMA DRM v2.0 [1] is an open standard developed by Open Mobile Alliance. The scope of OMA Digital Rights Management covers all aspects of controlling the distribution and consumption of digital media objects. We are given the ability to manage previews of content, to enable superdistribution (a method of digital content distribution where the content is distributed to consumers by other consumers) of DRM Content, and also to enable transfer of content between DRM Agents. Apart from that, the OMA DRM specification provides a mechanism for secure DRM Agent authentication as well as for secure packaging and distribution of content and usage rights related to the content. To sum it all up, OMA DRM manages the entire content lifecycle.

Figure 6.1 illustrates the functional architecture of OMA DRM, presenting all the functional entities playing specific roles in the DRM system.

The following functional entities have been identified in the architecture:

- **DRM Agent:** a trusted entity within the device, responsible for enforcing permission and constraints associated with DRM Content, thus controlling access to the content.
- **Content Issuer:** an entity that delivers DRM Content; the format of the DRM Content and the way it is delivered to a DRM Agent is also defined by OMA DRM.
- **Rights Issuer:** an entity that assigns permissions and constraints to DRM Content, and generates Rights Objects; a Rights Object is an XML document expressing permissions and constraints associated with a piece of DRM Content.

- **User:** a person accessing the content; the user can only access DRM Content through a DRM Agent.
- **Off-device storage:** as DRM Content is inherently secure, it may be stored by users off-device, for example for backup purposes; adequate Rights Objects containing only stateless permissions may also be stored in the same way.

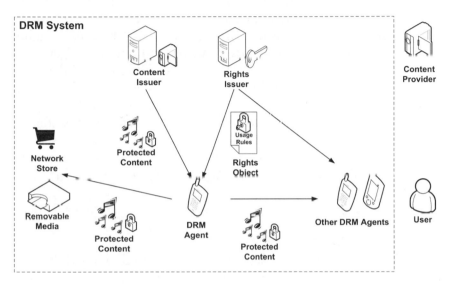

Figure 6.1   OMA DRM functional architecture [1]

Before the content is delivered, it is packaged and thus protected from unauthorized access. The content is packaged into DCF (DRM Content Format), a secure content package for the encrypted content. Not only does it contain the secured data, but it also carries additional information such as content description, Rights Issuer URI (from where the Rights Object can be obtained) and much more. This additional information is not encrypted and is available to everyone.

In order to unlock the DRM Content inside the DCF, the Content Encryption Key (CEK) is required. This key is contained within a Rights Object, an XML document issued by the Rights Issuer. In respect to this, the DRM Content cannot be used without the corresponding Rights Object, and can only be used according to the permissions and restrictions (how many times the content can be viewed, period of time when we are allowed to access the content) specified in the Rights Object. Moreover, the Rights Object is generated for the dedicated content and also for the specific target DRM Agent. The sensitive parts of the Rights Object, such as the CEK, are protected using a Rights Encryption Key (REK) and only this target Agent can access the Rights Object, and thus the CEK.

At the point of consumption, the Rights Objects have to be enforced while accessing the DRM Content. This is achieved by introducing the DRM Agent, a trusted component of the device. The agent is responsible for handling all the restrictions and permissions for the content on the device. Also, as we stated before, a Rights Object is bound to a specific DRM Agent, and only that agent can access it. As the content cannot be accessed without a valid Rights Object, it can be freely distributed, enabling superdistribution (users' exchange of content). When a user receives the content this way, in order to access it, he/she has to purchase an adequate Rights Object.

Since both the DCF and the Rights Object are inherently secure, they can be delivered using any transport mechanism, including pull (HTTP Pull, OMA Download), push (WAP Push, MMS) and streaming.

Some of the possible supported usage scenarios and models are as follows:

- **Basic pull model:** a user selects the content to download, browsing some web page, the content issuer protects the content and the Rights Issuer generates the Rights Object for the content and the target DRM Agent; the Rights Object includes permissions as defined during the purchase transaction.
- **Push of DRM Content:** the content is pushed directly to a device using, for example, MMS, without a preceding discovery process.
- **Streaming of DRM Content:** the content is packetized and delivered as a stream; in this case the stream itself is protected.
- **Backup:** the content can be stored safely on a removable medium as it can be accessed only by a particular DRM Agent using an associated Rights Object; Rights Objects can also be stored, apart from those containing stateful permissions.
- **Superdistribution:** free distribution of content; in order to access the content, a new Rights Object must be purchased.
- **Export:** the content can be exported to other DRM systems.
- **Unconnected device support:** a connected device can act as an intermediary to assist an unconnected device to purchase and download content and Rights Objects.

6.2   WINDOWS MEDIA DRM 10

Windows Media DRM 10 [2] for Portable Devices, one of the versions of Windows Media DRM, is an easy-to-implement, lightweight technology developed by the Microsoft Corporation. Generally, it is a platform enabling protection and secure content delivery for playback on computers, portable terminals and network devices. As far as portable terminals are concerned, both storing and playback of audio and video content from the local hard drive and playback of video-on-demand content over a broadcast network are supported. It is worth mentioning that the technology is not only restricted to Windows-based devices; all that is required is the manufacturer signing a license agreement with Microsoft.

The system is very flexible, accommodating most of the existing real-life business scenarios. Moreover, it is under constant development (as there is always an assumption that it may be cracked), introducing newer and newer features and addressing rapidly emerging needs. First, let us look at the benefits from the content owner's point of view. The main advantage, apart from the root function of protecting the digital media content, is that the existing content will not have to be re-encoded. The files are just packaged with robust encryption algorithms and then can be either streamed or downloaded directly to the consumer's device. Content service providers can, however, experiment with different business models without worrying about losses caused by insufficient protection. This can open a potentially big market, as the possibility of easily transferring the content acquired through subscription services to other devices exists.

It is also important to notice that although protecting the content is crucial, an excessive protection scheme should not impact upon user satisfaction. With Windows Media DRM 10, the consumer is able to easily find, acquire and play the content anywhere and at any time. Through this, we also understand providing a simple way of transferring the content as well as corresponding rights to or from the portable device (or any other device).

Some currently supported business and license acquisition scenarios are:

- **Direct license acquisition:** a license can be directly acquired using the cellular access uplink/downlink channel.

- **Subscription services:** it is possible to transfer content and the corresponding licenses to the device of the user's choice.
- **Rental services:** the consumer rents a movie and can watch it within the next, say, 24 hours.
- **Preview and purchase content:** consumers are offered the chance to preview songs before buying them; they are allowed to download any song and play it only two times, after that they are given instructions on how to purchase the item.
- **Protection of sensitive materials:** some materials can be viewed only once and after that become inaccessible.

To sum it all up, Windows Media DRM 10 has, amongst others, the following properties: it establishes the number of times the content can be played, specifies the validity time of the content (after that it cannot be viewed), enables transfer of content along with the licenses to different devices, handles copy permissions (also burning to CDs), and many more.

6.3   IPSEC

The IPsec (Internet Protocol security) protocol [3] is one of the most common solutions used for security purposes where IPDC is concerned. Designed to provide security for the IP layer, it is easy to implement since IPDC is an IP-based technology. It provides the following services: access control, connectionless integrity, data origin authentication, rejection of replayed packets, encryption and limited traffic flow confidentiality. All these services are IP-layer-based, thus higher level protocols can use them as well.

Encapsulation is the basis of IPsec. An original, unsecured IP packet is encrypted and wrapped into IPsec packets by adding the IPsec header information. In this condition, the secured packet is transmitted.

Security Association (SA) is the main concept of IPsec. It is a set of security services, dependent on the selected protocol, mode, endpoints and the choice of optional services within the protocol. In IPDC, SA works in the transport mode, resulting in a security association between hosts. The tunnel mode is also available and is essentially an SA applied to an IP tunnel. This mode shall not be used in IPDC, though. The structure of the encapsulated packet depends on security protocol selection. SA supports two security protocols:

AH (Authentication Header) and ESP (Encapsulating Security Payload). The AH provides data integrity only, while the ESP provides data integrity and confidentiality as well. Therefore, in IPDC, ESP is used. IPsec provides many different security options, supporting many different algorithms. However, only a small group is used in IPDC implementation. All of them can be found in the detailed specification [4].

Figure 6.2 is the basis for the Security Association instantiation process description. When the Key Stream Message is delivered to the

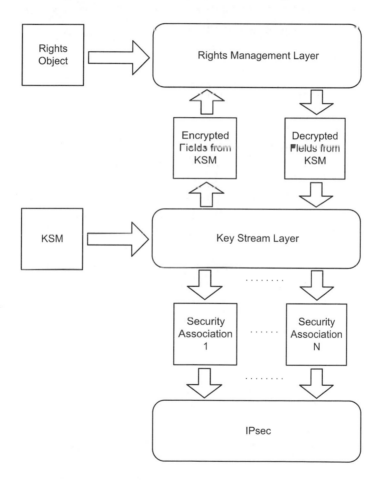

KSM: Key Stream Message
Ipsec: Internet Protocol Security

Figure 6.2 IPsec Security Association elements [4]

Key Stream Layer, it is decrypted by the Rights Management Layer using Rights Objects information. Using the available information (data and the encrypted key), the Key Stream Layer instantiates the Security Association. Security Association is uniquely identified by a triple consisting of a Security Parameter Index (SPI) carried by an ESP header, an IP Destination Address and a security protocol identifier (ESP or AH).

IPsec is the main content and data stream protection method, thus it shall be supported by all available terminals. While it can be used to provide security in applications other than IPDC, cooperation with other IPsec implementations is necessary.

6.4   SECURE REAL-TIME TRANSPORT PROTOCOL

The Secure Real-Time Transport Protocol (SRTP) [5] is a profile of the Real-Time Transport Protocol (RTP), which provides message integrity and authentication, confidentiality and replay protection to the RTP traffic, as well as to the RTCP (Real-Time Transport Control Protocol) control traffic. It operates at the session layer and supports both unicast and multicast applications. SRTP intercepts RTP packets and then forwards an equivalent SRTP packet on the sending side, and intercepts SRTP packets and passes an equivalent RTP packet up the stack on the receiving side. It can achieve a high throughput and low packet expansion and is considered a suitable protection for heterogeneous environments, such as, for example, the IPDC network.

The main goals of SRTP are:

- ensuring confidentiality of the RTP payload;
- ensuring integrity of the entire RTP packet, together with protection against replayed packets;
- limited packet expansion to preserve the bandwidth and reduce costs;
- ensuring independence from the underlying transport, network and physical layers used by RTP (high tolerance to packet loss and re-ordering).

Besides the above-mentioned goals, SRTP provides other features, aimed at further enhancing the security, including the single 'master key' (random bit string). The 'session keys' are provided by the key derivation function and are derived in a cryptographically secure way from the 'master key'. Thus, the key management protocol needs to exchange only one master key, all the necessary session keys are generated by applying the key derivation function. In addition, to further increase the security, the key derivation can be configured to periodically refresh the session keys, which limits the amount of ciphertext produced by a fixed key, available for an adversary to cryptanalyze.

For encryption and decryption of the data flow, only one default cipher has been specified. This is called AES (Advanced Encryption Standard) and can be used in the following two modes, which turn the original block AES cipher into a stream cipher:

- **Segmented integer counter mode:** allows random access to any blocks, which is essential for the RTP traffic running over an unreliable network. In the role of 'counter' almost any function can be used, provided that it does not repeat for a large number of iterations. Typically, an ordinary integer incremental counter is applied. This mode is the default encryption algorithm with the default encryption key length of 128 bits and the default session salt key (the 'salting' keys technique is used to protect against precomputation and time–memory tradeoff attacks) length of 112 bits.
- **f8-mode:** developed to encrypt UMTS 3G mobile network data. It is a variation of Output Feedback Mode, enhanced to be searchable and with a more elaborate initialization function. The encryption key and salt key values are as above.

It is worth mentioning that SRTP has the ability to disable encryption, which is denoted as using the 'NULL cipher'. It does not perform any encryption; the input stream is just copied to the output stream. It can be used when the confidentiality guarantees ensured by SRTP are not required, while other SRTP features (such as authentication and message integrity) may be used.

However, the described encryption itself does not secure the message integrity. The data can be forged by an attacker or the previously transmitted data can be replayed. To address these weaknesses, the SRTP standard provides means to enable authentication, secure the integrity of data and safety from replay. To authenticate the message and to protect its integrity, the HMAC-SHA1 algorithm (Keyed-Hashing for Message Authentication; for more details refer to [6]) is incorporated. However, this does not protect against replay attacks. In order to introduce replay protection the receiver must maintain the indices of previously received messages. These are then compared with the index of each new received message and the new message is admitted only if it has not been played before. Here we have to put strong stress on message integrity protection, as otherwise the message indices can be easily spoofed.

6.5   ISMACRYPT

Using ISMACrypt (Internet Streaming Media Alliance Encryption and Authentication) [4] is another way of securing transmissions in IPDC. The specification defines use of the RTP/MPEG (Real-Time Transport Protocol/Moving Picture Experts Group) protocol for the data plane, and use of SDP (Session Description Protocol) as well as RTSP (Real-Time Streaming Protocol) for the control plane. Thus, ISMACrypt is an application layer security system. It provides end-to-end protection and is truly universal. It can be applied to various key management, security and DRM systems.

The IPDC implementation of the ISMACrypt system shall use the default cipher, mode and configuration. Moreover, the key should change over time; however, not faster than once a second. Figure 6.3 shows the key management process of ISMACrypt. The Key Stream Message consists of ISMACryptKey and ISMACryptKeyIndicator parameters. They are both encrypted. The Key Stream Layer, using the Rights Management Layer, decrypts the key information and sends it to the content decrypter. The ISMACryptKeyIndicator is responsible for ISMACryptKey allocation to the content stream in the receiver. The ISMACryptSalt parameter is used to signal the ISMACrypt salt in the attributes of each encrypted media stream. All IPDC devices should support ISMA Encryption and Authentication.

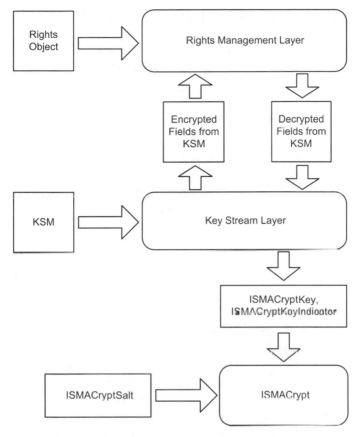

KSM: Key Stream Message
ISMACrypt: Internet Streaming Media Alliance Encryption and Authentication

Figure 6.3 ISMACrypt key management [4]

6.6 DVB CONDITIONAL ACCESS

Along with the previously described systems, the DVB-CA (Conditional Access) system has been developed and specified especially for use in digital broadcast networks, including IPDC. It defines a common scrambling algorithm and a common interface for accessing the scrambled content. System providers may develop their proprietary conditional access systems based on these specifications.

6.7   LIMITATIONS OF DRM SYSTEMS

It is obvious that Digital Rights Management systems are essential for the protection of copyright content distributed in a digital form through broadcast and multicast networks. Without proper protection, the content could be freely redistributed once it was acquired from the content providers. In such a situation, the whole business could become unprofitable or, at the very least, the revenues would be significantly reduced. This is something the content providers and distributors cannot accept.

However, there are still several problems concerning DRM systems, which need to be solved. The first issue is the interoperability between the different existing Digital Rights Management standards. In principle, all of these systems encrypt the content so that only eligible users may access it. Such an encryption also specifies the rules which govern the distribution and use of the content. For example, it may be specified on which device the content may be viewed, whether it may be copied to some external drive and, finally, whether it may be further distributed and on what conditions. Due to some business arrangements, several groups backing up different standards have formed on the market. This leads to the situation where different content providers, in order to protect their content during distribution, use different formats and DRM systems. A very good example here is the Apple iTunes store. The songs purchased from iTunes cannot be played using other players because of the lack of interoperability between the existing DRM systems. In particular, one would have to cope with different file formats, usage licenses and different requirements on the capabilities of the devices and installed software. A similar problem would occur if we wanted to access content purchased from some other online store using Apple devices. Unfortunately, the situation may get even more complicated in the near future as more and more companies enter the multimedia distribution business and usually tend to support their own proprietary Digital Rights Management system.

The second issue concerns the security and robustness of the DRM systems themselves. The rapid evolution of computing technologies has led to a situation whereby every code and every system sooner or later will be broken. This problem is even more serious when we realize that the pace at which the DRM systems evolve is significantly slower than the pace of technological progress. And as interest in content of a high popularity or value will also increase, more and more effort will be made to break the system. In this context, it is essential to design as robust systems as possible and renew the DRM systems once they are broken.

The second problem may be solved by developing more advanced and sophisticated DRM standards based on algorithms which are difficult to break. Still, we have to remember that a Digital Rights Management system cannot be too complicated or CPU-intensive, as the secured and encrypted content needs then to be decrypted by the end device. And the device is usually mobile, with a relatively low computing power and limited battery life.

Solving the interoperability problem is far more difficult as it requires cooperation between the parties behind the different standards. As a result of such cooperation, open, international and widely accepted and supported standards could emerge. This would allow delivery of any content and consumption at any time and place, using any available device. One of the organizations promoting the interoperability between DRM technologies for consumer devices and services is the Coral Consortium founded in 2004 [7]. Coral focuses on defining a service delivery architecture that would allow existing DRM systems to co-exist. The consortium also aims at providing standard protocols and interface specifications, which would enable interoperability between different content formats, service platforms and devices [8].

Finally, let us get back to the issue of securing the multimedia content. In the most common scenario the digital data is secured by applying an encryption scheme. Using a secret encryption key, the content is ciphered and may be deciphered only by a user having a correct decrypting key. The problem here is that the users may illegally distribute the decrypting keys and in such a situation the whole system simply would not work. A remedy here would be to use biometric authentication (e.g., fingerprints, retina scans, voice). Devices with an in-built fingerprint sensor are already on the market (see Figure 6.4).

Traditional encryption schemes may be used with biometric data or the biometric data may be used to generate keys used in content protection frameworks. The main advantage of biometric authentication is that the biometric data is not that easy to share with third parties, unlike, for example, passwords.

Figure 6.4   Fujitsu FOMA F905i mobile phone with an in-built fingerprint sensor (reproduced by permission of Fujitsu Limited)

REFERENCES

[1]   Open Mobile Alliance, *DRM Architecture*, OMA-AD-DRM-V2_0-20060303-A, Approved Version 2.0 – 03 Mar 2006.

[2]   Microsoft Corporation, *Digital Rights Management (DRM)*, http://www.microsoft.com/windows/windowsmedia/forpros/drm/default.mspx, 2 February 2006.

[3]   RFC 2401 (S. Kent and R. Atkinson), *Security Architecture for the Internet Protocol*, November 1998.

[4]   DVB Document A100, *IP Datacast over DVB-H: Service Purchase and Protection (SPP)*, http://www.dvb-h.org, December 2005.

[5]   RFC 3711 (M. Baugher, D. McGrew, M. Naslund, E. Carrara and K. Norrman), *The Secure Real-time Transport Protocol (SRTP)*, March 2004.

[6]   RFC 2104 (H. Krawczyk, M. Bellare and R. Canetti), *HMAC: Keyed-Hashing for Message Authentication*, February 1997.

[7]   Coral Consortium, *An Overview*, http://www.coral-interop.org, February 2006.

[8]   W. Zeng, H. Yu and C.-Y. Lin, *Multimedia Security Technologies for Digital Rights Management*, Elsevier (Academic Press), Amsterdam, 2006.

7

Business Model

A promising technology remains only a promising technology if there is no support from the business world. With both IPDC and MBMS this should not be an issue, as all the parties engaged will benefit once the system is implemented and the services launched.

Services such as mobile TV, which here will be treated as a model service, offer attractive market opportunities for all. But to make it possible, the telecommunications, media and broadcasting industries need to cooperate, exploiting each other's core competencies. The main actors involved in implementing IP Datacast services include cellular network operators, broadcast network operators, TV broadcasters and media companies. In the case of MBMS the list is shorter and lacks the broadcast network operators. Of course, we must not forget about the vendors, who will supply the handsets capable of handling the services and other networking equipment, building up the network infrastructure. In addition to this, there are also the software vendors. After all, no hardware can operate without operating systems and no services can be accessed without appropriate applications.

Figure 7.1 shows a generic business value chain. The three roles common to both IPDC and MBMS have been presented. They are accompanied by the intermediate components, which are different for the mentioned technologies (on the diagram shown as a dashed-line box). Further, in this chapter, all the common roles as well as those specific to each technology, will be discussed.

Multimedia Broadcasting and Multicasting in Mobile Networks
G. Iwacz, A. Jajszczyk and M. Zajączkowski
© 2008 John Wiley & Sons, Ltd

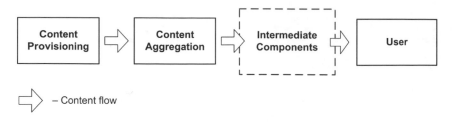

Figure 7.1   Generic business value chain

7.1   COMMON COMPONENTS

As presented in Figure 7.1, there are basically three components in the value chain common to IPDC and MBMS. First, we have the content providers. Their role, when considering mobile television, remains pretty much the same as for traditional broadcasting. With only limited additional costs they gain a new distribution channel offering existing or specially prepared content. For example, FOX Entertainment Group, apart from offering the shows from its archives, already provides short mobile episodes (dubbed 'mobisodes') of its popular 24 series. Following this, other content providers such as Comedy Central and MTV have chosen similar strategies in developing content exclusively for the mobile environment.

Moreover, in the case of mobile TV, completely new audiences can be reached; namely active people that are not present at home in front of their TV sets. TV can be brought into streets, buses, waiting rooms, parks – simply wherever we want. All of this results in the creation of a brand new format for popular TV shows as well as the evolution of new prime times (e.g., commuting periods and lunchtime). It is worth noting that not all of the already existing TV shows are equally predestined to be offered to mobile users. As the users tend to tune into mobile TV for short periods of time (morning commuting, waiting in a line), the offered content should also be adequately short and preferably should constitute a closed entity. In such cases, the user can start watching at any moment while still understanding what it is all about. Some types of appropriate shows are:

- news;
- weather forecasts;
- short cartoons;

- business information (e.g., stock quotations);
- music programs (showing video clips).

The TV shows are additionally assisted by a set of accompanying services. Users can, for example, download a ring tone based on the leading tune of a show or access an online shop with items related to the show. Of course, there is also some content prepared for a wide set of services other than mobile TV. These are mainly the services that are already offered to cellular network subscribers by the specialized media houses. Examples of the content here include:

- ring tones;
- wallpapers;
- games;
- 'what's on' at the nearby cinema;
- video-on-demand (VoD);
- mp3s;
- localized information.

To summarize, the key benefits for the content providers are listed below:

- **New audiences:** content providers easily reach new audiences without even knowing their identities and regardless of their physical location. These are often people who do not watch TV at all but at the same time are perfect targets for the advertisers.
- **New distribution channels:** an opportunity arises to distribute content through additional distribution channels and thus monetize the existing content libraries.
- **Market for new types of specific content designed for the mobile environment:** content providers gain the opportunity to produce content specifically designed for the mobile environment (small screen, short watching periods). In the beginning, content from popular sources may be adapted to mobile conditions. However, as time goes by, the content delivered will evolve into something that is optimized for mobile consumption.
- **Revenue without serious investment:** this is because the business model relies on the operator's network services (charging/billing, security, DRM).

- **Pay-per-download content:** content providers may offer certain content on a pay-per-download basis. For content that is not normally distributed in such a way (e.g., music, video clips or TV shows), mobile distribution networks may provide an additional monetization channel.
- **Additional revenue streams:** content providers can earn money by outsourcing one-to-many content delivery (e.g., to companies interested in advertising their products and services, which are also related to a specified user's location).
- **Access to archives:** providing access to content archives may provide further revenue opportunities. At no additional cost, content removed from primary circulation may be offered to users and generate significant revenue.

Next, we have the content aggregators, who buy content from different content providers and then sell it through various distribution channels. Users pay for subscriptions, which give them access to the content, offered usually in bundles. For aggregators, IP Datacast or MBMS again create a new media distribution channel, reaching people while on the move. This role can be easily carried out either by a cellular service provider (sometimes a cellular network operator) or a datacasting services provider.

Finally, we have the reason for all of this: the user. Thanks to introducing IPDC and MBMS services, such as mobile TV, into mobile devices, consumers are not restricted by time and place. Anywhere they are, at any time, they can tune in to watch their favorite show. They can enjoy new content and services on a new level, not only passively, but also experiencing full interactivity. The list of benefits is long and grows very quickly as new ideas for services based on the new technologies evolve. Some of these are:

- receiving appealing streaming content (also real-time);
- paying only one common bill for all services;
- accessing new services wherever we are, at all times;
- receiving the content on all user devices (meaning that the content can be transferred from one device to another, of course with respect to Digital Rights Management);
- preparing the content according to the user's preferences and location.

7.2 COMPONENTS SPECIFIC TO IPDC

The components common to both IPDC and MBMS have been described in the previous section. Those related strictly to IPDC are presented in Figure 7.2.

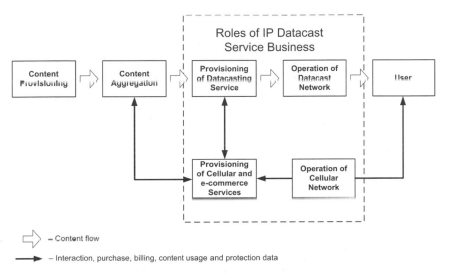

Figure 7.2 IPDC value chain [1]

The datacast service provider controls distribution of the datacast capacity. Usually, content aggregators buy the capacity directly, either as a long-term agreement for broadcasting annual content or on special occasions to deliver particular content at agreed times (e.g., World Championships). An IP Datacast service provider also takes care of ensuring the protection of available content from illegal viewing. Moreover, in addition to capacity, the datacast service provider controls the Electronic Service Guide. The guide is broadcast along with the content, providing users with information as to which shows and services are available, and at what times. For the consumer, the guide is simply a key to accessing the service, without which watching a show would be just a lucky guess. Thanks to mobile TV, service providers also benefit, obtaining new revenue streams such as advertising and subscriptions.

Next, we have datacast network operators. They own and operate the whole digital broadcasting infrastructure, including mast sites, transmitters, etc. Often, they also happen to be the frequency license holders. Consequently, the companies operating datacast services purchase capacity and coverage from them. One network operator can sell capacity to many service operators, which makes it cost effective. Additionally, by implementing IP Datacast services themselves, the datacast network operators gain an opportunity to generate additional growth from their investment in the digital television infrastructure. Actually, in practice, the two above-mentioned roles are quite often combined.

The next two components described are also present for MBMS, but here these will be considered in the context of IPDC. First, we have the mobile network operators, who will be able to provide interactivity via their networks' return channels (polls, online voting). Additionally, they will offer billing and e-commerce services to partners, which will generate new revenue streams for them. After all, since the cellular operators already are in possession of large customer databases, it is easiest for them to charge for the services. Following this, a customer receives only a single bill, which is obviously convenient. The cellular network operators also benefit in many other ways. First of all, they will offer their customers a completely new and desirable service, including mobile TV and all the others described in the previous section. Secondly, the revenues will grow thanks to the increased traffic in the network via the return channel (content purchasing, data and web-based services). Finally, to fully exploit the possibilities, the cellular companies may consider building and operating the IP Datacast network, which should considerably enhance their profits.

The cellular and e-commerce service provider offers the access necessary for purchasing the content and experiencing the available interactive services. All of this is possible thanks to cooperation with a cellular operator; therefore, it is possible that it will cover this role as well. By provision of e-commerce services we mean selling users access rights to the content (for example, in the form of monthly subscriptions). At the same time, all consumer purchase actions are recorded and passed to a billing system. The revenues are then shared with other parties. Some of the services offered by the cellular service provider can employ only cellular networks. After all, it is not always worthwhile and justifiable to use the broadcast network. This group of services includes mainly those aimed at a particular user (one-to-one services). Examples here would be video-on-demand or purchasing wallpapers or ring tones related to watched TV shows.

7.3   COMPONENTS SPECIFIC TO MBMS

In the case of MBMS, the role of a cellular network operator is similar to the role of a datacast network operator. It also owns the infrastructure, holds the licenses and sells network capacity to different service providers. Here it is worth reminding ourselves that the implementation of the MBMS technology requires only minor changes to the infrastructure of the existing cellular networks; only one additional component (the BM-SC) is needed. This reduces the start-up costs, while the potential benefits are very promising.

The business models for the broadcast and multicast modes of MBMS are different, though related. In the broadcast mode the information from, for example, tourist or emergency services is sent to all users within a certain area. It can be employed, for instance, to send movie previews in order to persuade users to visit a movie theater near the users' location. The users usually receive these services free of charge. In some cases, the content provider can pay for the service itself, so that the users are able to receive the content (advertisements). Additionally, these kinds of free services increase traffic in the network, which makes them profitable for the operator. The services in the multicast mode, on the other hand, are typically subscription-based. Here, the user has to activate the service (paying a charge) in order to be able to access it. An example here would be subscribing to receive top-rated goals from the Champions' League.

Based on what was presented above, the following three business scenarios can be derived:

- **Free-to-air broadcast:** this kind of service creates the possibility of attracting users and stimulating subscriptions to other services, for which the user will be charged.
- **Subscription-based services (broadcast or multicast):** this reverse-charging model is thought to be the most appropriate for MBMS services. Here, the revenue is shared between the operators and content providers (also content aggregators) based on user charges.
- **Offering potential multicast services at lower prices:** network load, generated by services realized by point-to-point and also by point-to-multipoint, may be lowered by introducing multicast. Thanks to multicast, popular services may then be offered at a lower price, which will further stimulate their usage without increasing the cost in the network [2].

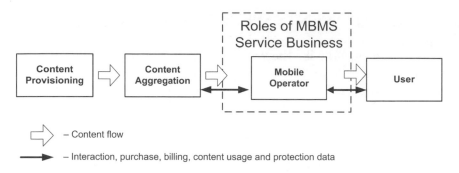

Figure 7.3   MBMS value chain

Figure 7.3 presents the MBMS services value chain. The operator can easily position itself in the center point of the value chain, thanks to the services only it can offer and also thanks to the information it possesses. The advantageous position of the operator stems from the following facts:

- **Billing system:** the operator has primary control over the billing system necessary to monetize the mobile TV services. The operator can handle many different billing models existing in today's mobile networks: pay-per-view, pay-per-content, pay-per-duration, post- and prepaid, discounts, etc.
- **Customer database:** the operator is in possession of the database of all its customers, which allows it to easily charge users for the consumed services. A customer receives only one bill and there is no need to spend additional money on the billing system, as it is already there.
- **Marketing:** a critical component that will for sure determine the success of mobile television services is customer awareness. As the mobile operators already have wide experience in this field, they will likely play an important role in marketing the new type of service and in educating the end-users in how to use the service.
- **Handset subsidies:** by employing the subsidizing mechanism the operators stimulate the process of handset exchange, which then has a major influence on adoption of new services on the market, particularly in their initial stages of deployment. This is so because without relatively modern terminals, the usage of new services is not possible. This is even more true when we consider mobile television, as here the handsets need, amongst other things,

a new radio receiver. Following this, without carriers' subsidies on handsets, it would be very difficult to achieve the pricing points necessary to help drive mass commercial adoption of mobile TV services.

Some of the benefits for the mobile operator include:

- it can acquire new customers, tempted by the additional services it is offering;
- the MBMS services promote on-demand traffic (higher revenues thanks to the traffic caused by the services);
- acting as a content aggregator it can buy services from content providers and then sell them in bundles;
- it can offer services to hotspots and corporate networks (e.g., private wireless local area networks) [3].

Still, the mobile operators need to evaluate and choose the right model for deploying mobile TV services in order to:

- maximize their network investment on cellular technologies;
- differentiate their service offering;
- maximize possible revenue.

7.4 TERMINALS AND NETWORK INFRASTRUCTURE

Aside from all the described roles and components, we must mention the handset manufacturers (along with handset component suppliers) and software vendors. Actually, without the appropriate devices, none of the services described earlier would be possible. In the case of MBMS, in contrast to IPDC, the existing terminals (mobile phones) can be used. Of course, we mean phones with color displays of a decent size and with all the necessary software, such as movie players, installed. While mobile TV is not actually tied to 3G networks, one may say that the service requires the enhanced functionality of the 3G-capable handset in order to deliver a perfectly suited mobile entertainment experience. Features such as faster data processing, an intuitive and enhanced user interface, increased operational memory and storage, all managed by a state-of-the-art efficient operating system are core components of a next generation handset contributing to a satisfactory user experience.

On the other side, although IPDC requires terminals to be equipped with additional receivers, the introduction of this technology into cell phones seems natural. After all, users will always appreciate carrying one device less. The new set of services will increase the attractiveness of mobile devices, triggering customers to switch to new terminals, thus providing a new source of revenue to manufacturers. Actually, the cost of the additional components, which need to be added to enable mobile TV functions on a handset (including antenna and RF components), is estimated to be not that high and should be around 10 to 15 euros. When we additionally compare this against the average price of a 3G handset, we can easily see that this additional cost is practically imperceptible and thus may be neglected.

As the devices will incorporate this new set of functions, from now on we may talk about so-called *terminal convergence*. The terminal must be able to access all the different radio networks simultaneously, especially the broadcast networks, in addition to the standard cellular ones (e.g., conducting a voice call using a cellular network and at the same time watching a TV show broadcast over a DVB-H network). Figure 7.4 presents the main success factors for a future terminal. These include a user-centric interface, portable intelligence and service convergence.

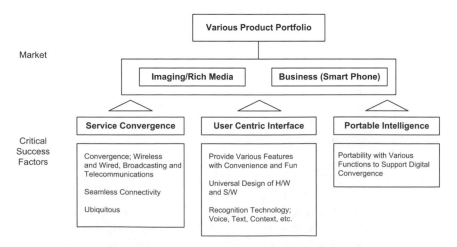

Figure 7.4   Success factors for future terminals [4]

Services are bound to be the driver for the future market and the technology will be just a means of providing the services for which the users will be willing to pay. When talking about existing telecommunications systems, we must agree that services were developed around the capabilities of the employed technology. In order to meet user expectations, next generation systems shall be service-driven; in other words, the technology will follow services and applications. In particular, the availability of high data rates is important, but at the same time meaningless if there are no services or applications to fully exploit this possibility.

One way of satisfying the consumers is to work on the convergence of services, from those originating from digital broadcasting to the commercial ones offered by cellular networks. However, introducing services that will be appealing to users is an extremely difficult task. One of the approaches is based on trying to map real-life situations with possible services that could help with making the users' lives more comfortable (e.g., location-aware services). Also, the services should have the following set of common features valued by users [4]:

- **user friendliness:** easy-to-use, simple and intuitive interfaces;
- **user personalization:** the possibility to configure the service according to the user's preferences;
- **network heterogeneity:** seamlessly offering continuous and pervasive services with a guaranteed QoS;
- **terminal heterogeneity:** supporting a wide scope of communication devices, from simple ones with limited capabilities to high-performance terminals crossing the borders between device types.

In order to support a wide set of services, terminals are becoming more and more complex. That is why it is important that designers should, in the first place, ensure a friendly, intuitive, user-centric interface, including features such as speech or handwriting recognition. These features, however, cannot negatively impact the terminal's portability, as this is one of its most important properties.

Portable intelligence refers to the schemes and techniques incorporated into the mobile terminal and its operating system that utilize the features offered by surrounding wireless networks to facilitate context awareness, decision making, location awareness and user profile awareness. One of the decisions taken is to which network the terminal should connect at a particular time (choosing the best way to accommodate the user's needs). Additionally, as the amount of data available in all networks is massive, it is not possible to capture every aspect of it. The terminal's role is to collect the data, interpret it and exchange it in a way that adapts to the user's context [5].

A single terminal that satisfies the needs of all users simply does not exist. Some customers are satisfied with a simple device equipped only with a set of basic features, while others aim at terminals supporting rich multimedia services. At this point, flexible, multimode terminals supporting a variety of functions seem to be the best candidates to gain the biggest market share. However, simple, single-mode terminals or specialized devices such as smart-phones will also have their advocates. Thus, the market for terminals can again be described by the word *heterogeneity*; there will be an appropriate terminal for everyone.

There are, however, some features that should be more carefully developed in the context of future terminals in contrast to the existing ones. They include [4]:

- high performance;
- multifunction;
- low power consumption;
- internetworking capability;
- wide bandwidth;
- miniaturization.

In particular, the power consumption has to be considered carefully. Because of the new multimedia applications, several active radio interfaces, large color displays and the necessary processing power, today's battery technology will be insufficient for future devices. Even if the terminal has extraordinary functions, these will not be appealing to users if the operational time of the device is very short. Some initiatives have been already taken; however, it will still be some time before new power sources will become commercially available and will be able to fulfill all needs. One promising technology in this field seems to be the Direct Methanol Fuel Cell (DMFC); however, we still have some time to wait before this kind of battery powers cell phones.

When we think about it, terminals can be regarded as one of the key factors in successful technology deployment. Without a small and handy device with a relatively large screen, none of the

Figure 7.5   Nokia 7710 with DVB-H receiver (reproduced by permission of © 2008 Nokia Corporation and © 2008 BBC)

new services would be attractive enough. Probably, one of the first devices designed to handle the IPDC technology was the Nokia 7710 terminal with a custom DVB-H receiver (Figure 7.5).

The terminal has only been available commercially without the built-in DVB-H receiver. In the meantime, Nokia proposed some new models (e.g., N92), designed especially for mobile TV reception. Moreover, currently Nokia sells stand-alone DVB-H receivers (Figure 7.6) that may be connected to Nokia mobile phones, transforming them into mobile TV terminals.

Brands like Samsung, Philips, Sagem and LG have also introduced their own DVB-H-enabled devices (e.g., the LG U960 device is offered in Italy). Of course, not only mobile phones can be used to access IPDC services, but every other device equipped with a DVB-H receiver. For example, PDAs with an external DVB-H receiver were used during the tests by the VTT Technical Research Centre of Finland.

After testing the TV service using the Nokia 7710 terminal at the Elisa Corporation premises, some observations were made. Audio/video quality was excellent and the compression was practically imperceptible. The screen size and resolution enable one to

Figure 7.6   Nokia SU-33W DVB-H receiver (reproduced by permission of © 2008 Nokia Corporation)

watch a regular TV channel and even to see and be able to read the subtitles clearly.

As indicated earlier in this section, the handset vendors themselves are very enthusiastic about the positive impact that the new services such as mobile TV may have on their business. In particular, the most important issue for the vendors is whether the potential new entertainment services will have an impact on replacement handset sales. The last couple of years have clearly shown that the integration of the right feature or functionality on a handset can materially spur replacement demand. An example here would be the strong replacement cycle started around 2003 with the introduction of color displays and then cameras into phones. This is why the handset vendors will likely follow this road and continue to enhance the capabilities of their products, introducing more media- and entertainment-related functionality in order to boost sales. Of course, we have to remember that here the situation is slightly different than it was when color displays and cameras were introduced. The market penetration of mobile TV handsets is dependent on the availability of mobile TV services, unlike a camera phone, which is not dependent on any service. Moreover, we also have to take into consideration the business model uncertainties and incremental cost for the service itself. Due to all of this, mobile TV is bound to have a slower adoption rate compared with the more rapid adoption of the aforementioned enhancements not dependent on service availability (e.g., music phones). Still, the process of handset replacement, even if it is not that extensive initially, will be very profitable for the vendors. When we take into consideration that today's mobile phones have a significantly longer lifespan than a couple of years ago (e.g., warranties extended from 12 to 24 or more months), we clearly see the reason for the urge to find new revenue streams. This then drives the introduction of more and more mobile TV capable terminals from which the user can choose.

While talking about handset vendors, we also have to mention handset component suppliers. The scope of components necessary to enable mobile television services on a handset can be divided into two main groups: primary components and secondary components. The primary components can be defined as the actual transmission and receiving circuits added to a handset (e.g., tuner, demodulator), which are indispensable for service delivery. On the other hand, we have the secondary components which are necessary to enhance the mobile TV experience. These are, for example, more powerful processors, memory or high-capacity batteries. As we can see, looking at today's 3G multimedia handsets, the support components have already been introduced, while the primary components are being specifically designed to enable mobile TV services.

Along with the new handsets, there is also a need for a new service provisioning infrastructure (mainly transmitters, servers and applications), required as the new services emerge. At the same time, the broadcast and cellular networks are bound to be enhanced while interest in the services increases. For example, additional transmitters and repeaters are necessary to provide high quality indoor reception [6].

Finally, we cannot forget about the software vendors. As always when a new complex technology is considered, there is a variety of software vendors that assist in enabling service deployment. These vendors can be found at several points on the mobile TV value chain, including billing, content distribution, user interface or Digital Rights Management applications. It is probable that many of these software applications will be delivered by the parties that also play other roles in the value chain, in order to accelerate the deployment of mobile TV (e.g., content providers, network operators). Still, other software vendors not necessarily related to the mobile TV business will likely try to gain a share of the market and capitalize on the market growth opportunity.

7.5 CHARGING SCENARIOS

As we have said in previous sections, all the functions related to billing will be carried out by the cellular network operator, as it already owns the necessary infrastructure. With the relevant billing system in place, next an appropriate charging scenario should be proposed. The options available here include:

- pay-per-view;
- pay-per-content;
- pay-per-duration;
- flat rate.

When we consider mobile TV, a flat-rate-based system would work best; this has been confirmed during several trials carried out worldwide. In this case, users would pay a constant monthly fee of a couple of euros for access to the basic set of channels. The fee itself would not be high; however, it would still be high enough to generate considerable revenue.

Apart from the basic set of channels, some extra ones would be available to users at an additional charge. When buying the premium monthly subscription, the user would gain access to all channels and could also receive some bonuses, such as a free hour of calls per day.

Along with mobile TV there is a set of additional services offered to users. Here, the other mentioned charging scenarios would be more appropriate, namely pay-per-view, pay-per-content or pay-per-duration. These services include downloading wallpapers, ring tones (also those related to watched TV shows), games, music video clips, etc. Here, the user would just pay a relevant fee for the requested content. As for the billing method, the service known as *premium*

SMS would probably be used in most cases. The charging process is as follows:

1. A user chooses the content he/she wishes to access and is asked to send a special premium SMS to the relevant number.
2. When the sent SMS is received by the service operator's system, a reply message is sent to the customer containing, for example, the activation code or the URL from where the content can be downloaded.
3. At the same time the service operator's system generates an appropriate EDR (Event Detail Record), which is then fed to the billing system. The charge is added to the monthly bill (or instantly deducted from the user's account in the case of a prepaid scenario).
4. Upon receiving the reply message, the customer can access the requested content.

As we can see, this process is really simple and intuitive. Additionally, and importantly, it lasts for only a couple of seconds, so the user gets access to the requested content practically immediately.

Of course, not only the premium SMS service can be used for making payments for ordered services. When we, for example, consider an online shop run by a mobile operator, the purchase process may be even easier. In this case, when the user browses the available content using the mobile device, he or she can make a purchase with a single click. After that the transaction has to be confirmed with another keyboard hit only. The confirmation phase is necessary here, otherwise we could potentially purchase something by mistake. Still, such 'shopping' is very quick; after only two clicks the service is available and the money is automatically deducted from the user account (prepaid scenario) or an appropriate EDR is generated and fed into the billing system.

Finally, we should not forget about the possibility of making a payment using our credit card. After all, today's mobile devices do not differ that much from computers. In the same way, purchasing services using them does not differ at all from buying products over the Internet. Therefore, after selecting the desired content, a user should just need to enter his/her credit card number. Access to the content is granted immediately and we do not need to worry about any bills, as the cost simply appears on our next card statement. Of course, the whole transaction is secured, just as it is when we make

Internet purchases. It can even be said that security is far higher. In the case of the Internet, everybody has access to the network and can easily intercept the data. It is only a matter of time and patience before the encryption is broken. On the other hand, when cellular networks are considered, because of their nature, no one actually can get access to the network to such an extent as with the Internet. As a result, cellular networks are more resistant to data interception and thus can be regarded as more secure.

7.6   SPECTRUM FOR MOBILE TV

Availability of radio spectrum is critical for all sectors using wireless communications including media, aviation and the telecommunications industry. However, for the telecom sector, spectrum standardization, spectrum allocation and spectrum availability are of the highest importance. The above is true for both operators and equipment vendors, for whom spectrum frequency harmonization has a huge impact on the business.

Despite several mobile TV solutions, including the emerging DVB-H, MBMS and DMB, the lack of spectrum may prevent the development of these platforms. It is a common belief that the issue of the availability of frequencies for mobile television needs to be addressed urgently in order to enable the launch of services as soon as possible. Furthermore, when we consider launch of DVB-H-based services, the most suitable frequencies are in the UHF broadcasting band (between 470 and 862 MHz), which is heavily utilized for analog and digital broadcasting. Although the number of available channels is increased thanks to digital transmission, spectrum will remain scarce until the analog switch-off time. It has to be remembered that this switchover from analog to digital television will not solve the problems automatically. The released spectrum needs to be harmonized carefully as widely as possible, both at the national and the international level. Actually, this will be a crucial moment in time. A carefully taken decision may boost development of new and exciting services, but at the same time incompetent regulations may jeopardize this chance. In other words, the decisions taken in the near future will have a lasting impact on the telecommunications, broadcasting and media industries.

As spectrum is a limited resource, service providers and operators behind different technologies have always paid close attention to allocation and standardization activities. The biggest challenge is to drive the standardization in such a way that all the existing technologies and the new, evolving ones are taken into account. This is why the allocation of spectrum should be a consultative process organized under a strong leadership; in particular, it should be coordinated at the international level. Within the structure of the ITU (International Telecommunication Union) we have a body responsible for management of the radio frequency spectrum called the ITU-R (ITU Radiocommunication Sector). Through a consultative process, frequencies are allocated for services based on various technologies: 3G, mobile television, (W)CDMA, digital television and wireless (WiFi, WiMAX). Apart from these, new standards emerge constantly and bring forth new requirements on the use of spectrum. As an outcome, globally harmonized bands are assigned to various services, still leaving specific allocation at a country level to the governments. Of course, in some cases there is a need to go beyond national borders to optimize the use of resources, secure noninterference, etc.

This consultative process at the international level has been effective, but also staggered in time, which does not align well with the nature of rapidly evolving services such as mobile television. The increasing need for spectrum and the urge to deploy services as soon as possible leads to a situation where country-specific approaches are quite common. Quite predictably, these do not always align with the global harmonization strategy. When we then remind ourselves that there are several standards, such as DVB-H and DMB, competing for the same spectrum resources, the situation is getting more and more complicated (refer to Figure 7.7).

When we consider all the technologies mentioned above, currently only GSM and CDMA-based technologies (e.g., UMTS) can benefit from a coordinated allocation of spectrum. This is all thanks to ITU activity and actually makes international roaming possible worldwide. But these technologies also generate demand for additional spectrum, as the number of subscribers is growing annually at a pace which could not have been foreseen a couple of years ago. This growth is accompanied by an ever-increasing number of multimedia services including mobile TV (unicast mode), which may be provided based on these technologies.

As we are aware, existing cellular networks are not perfectly suited for delivering mobile TV. In addition, broadcasters aimed to gain direct access to users' mobile terminals, so that mobile television

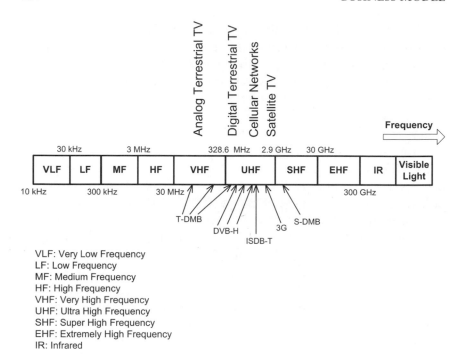

Figure 7.7   Mobile TV – use of spectrum

could be delivered without mediation by the cellular operators' side. And so the race for spectrum began. A good example here is the DVB-H standard and the lobby behind it. A clear aim backed up by a good campaign paid off and currently the spectrum for the technology is being allocated on a country-by-country basis. As this allocation process is moving forward, other standards focus on preallocated spectrum (e.g., services based on DMB are being deployed using the DAB spectrum meant for digital audio broadcasting). Of course, the existing transmission standards may not be used everywhere for delivery of high quality mobile TV, and it may take a while until common spectrum for mobile TV is allocated, as a result of a lengthy consultation process. Such a situation can be seen in the United States, where operators who rushed ahead with service launch had to rely on spectrum gained as a result of winning FCC (Federal Communications Commission) auctions. An example here would be the proprietary FLO standard (described in detail in Chapter 5), which uses the 700 MHz spectrum owned by MediaFLO (Qualcomm). Similarly, services based on DVB-H have been deployed on privately held spectrum, examples include HiWire (in the 700 MHz band) and Modeo (in the 1670 MHz band) [7].

If we take a closer look at Figure 7.7, we could say that there is plenty of spectrum available, so why not just assign a huge band explicitly for mobile television? But are all bands suitable for mobile TV? Unfortunately the answer is 'no', and the three factors determining this are: the Doppler effect, signal propagation losses and the in-building penetration loss. Additionally, the most suitable spectrum varies depending on the considered technology.

The Doppler effect is defined as the change in frequency and wavelength of a wave as perceived by an observer moving relative to the source of the wave. The shift in frequency is proportional to the velocity of the user and the frequency, so the higher the frequency, the higher the frequency shift, which limits the allowable receiver velocity.

Moving on to signal propagation losses, we see that these also increase with a growth in frequency, but this time the loss is proportional to the square of the frequency.

Finally, the in-building penetration losses also increase with the frequency. Moreover, higher frequencies require larger transmitter power. Based on this, it is obvious that very high frequencies are not the answer. Unfortunately, low frequencies (lower VHF bands) are not the best choice either. In this case, significantly larger antennas would have to be used to secure high quality reception. This would not sit well with today's principles of handheld design, where the aim is not only quality of services but also the 'look and feel' of the devices. So the choice made has to be a compromise between high and low frequencies. And here we have the VHF and UHF bands, but unfortunately these frequency bands are pretty much occupied (see Figure 7.7 for details). The UHF band would be best suited here, since the Doppler effect is not that high and mobile reception would be possible at velocities of up to 500 km/h. Unfortunately, due to the spectrum allocation for GSM 900 differing from country to country, this band will not necessarily be available. The issue of frequency allocation for mobile television is not that easy or straightforward.

One of the main advantages of DVB-H should be borne in mind. The costs involved in the service roll-out are minimized as DVB-H is designed to use the same spectrum and infrastructure as DVB-T. However, for each country, a part of the spectrum earmarked for digital terrestrial television (DVB-T) would still have to be explicitly reserved for DVB-H-based systems.

A similar situation exists with T-DMB, which is an extension of the DAB standards (see Chapter 5 for details). The primary reason for considering T-DMB is that systems based on this technology are designed to use the DAB spectrum, which was allocated some time ago in many countries. Services based on T-DMB have already been launched in Korea (2005) and in Germany.

After a given spectrum band has been reserved for some technology or service, the next step is the spectrum allocation process. In European countries, the most common approach has been spectrum auctions (auctioning the 60 MHz band divided into 5 MHz blocks). Spectrum was simply purchased by a company that proposed the highest bid. In another scenario, the spectrum remains in the hands of the government, and only a license to provide services using this spectrum is leased to service providers. The US approach is similar. In 2006, the Federal Communications Commission auctioned spectrum in the 2 GHz band (1710–1755 MHz and 2110–2155 MHz) to enable growth of wireless services such as mobile television. In contrast, in Korea no auctions have been organized and the spectrum is allocated on a fixed-fee basis.

ITU-R has done a lot in the field of spectrum harmonization and allocation for various emerging services. In particular, much work has been conducted under the aegis of WARC (World Administrative Radio Conference). WARC meetings are held periodically and the interval between them is usually used for industry consultations. The last WARC, in 2007, was focused on spectrum harmonization at an international level and on granting additional spectrum to rapidly developing services such as mobile television. More on the outcome of the conference may be found in the conference proceedings [8]. The proceedings gather together decisions taken at the conference, including the new and revised provisions for radio regulations and associated appendices, as well as the new and revised resolutions and recommendations adopted by the conference.

Apart from the international activities under the aegis of the ITU, a lot has been going on at the European level. In 2002, the European Commission (EC) issued the Radio Spectrum Decision [9], which, amongst other things, established the creation of the Radio Spectrum Committee (RSC) and the Radio Spectrum Policy Group (RSPG). These bodies were to assist the Commission in all decisions concerning spectrum harmonization. As an outcome of its work, at the end of 2005, the RSPG published a document on Wireless Access Policy for Electronic Communications Services (WAPECS) implications for electronic communications markets. Following this, in 2006, a review of the existing 2002 framework in the field of spectrum was initiated [10]. The new spectrum management policy rests on the following foundations, which aim to reduce barriers to market entry as much as possible [11]:

- Technology neutrality: any technology may be used in a given frequency band.
- Service neutrality: any service may be offered using a given spectrum band.
- Granting access to spectrum resources by trading the usage rights to optimize the efficiency and flexibility of usage.

Based on these principles, the European Commission aims to achieve spectrum commercialization before 2010, particularly in bands below 3 GHz. The RSPG recently issued an opinion referring to the introduction of multimedia services in bands allocated to broadcasting services [12]. In this document, the RSPG tries to influence the Commission to remove all the constraints in current licenses for fixed mobile as well as broadcasting services, which may prevent the development of mobile television services. However, as the market for mobile television and other emerging services is developing at such a fast pace (the forecast is 69 million global subscribers by 2009, generating revenue of 4 to 5 billion euros), the spectrum decisions cannot wait until 2010 and should be taken as soon as possible [11]. This especially refers to the harmonization of DVB-H bands around Europe and granting bands to other emerging services.

Based on the information in this section, it is apparent that at this moment, spectrum harmonization and allocation for mobile television are of crucial importance. This is especially significant as, currently, many cellular operators are ready to provide mobile TV services to their subscribers. Recently Klaus Hartmann, CEO of ERA PTC – a member of T-Mobile group and one of the biggest mobile operators in Poland – stated that the company is technically capable of providing a mobile television service based on the DVB-H standard. In other words, the service could be launched immediately. The only obstacle is the lack of spectrum allocation.

7.7 SUMMARY

As we can see, the described mobile television value chain has many complex layers and several parties involved, including content providers, aggregators, datacast network operators, equipment vendors (handsets and infrastructure), software providers and mobile operators. Because of this complex ecosystem, the possible success of mobile TV services will depend on solidifying the elaborated business models, as each and every party involved aims to maximize profits and take the market lead. Of course, there is also the issue of bandwidth availability. At the moment, harmonization and allocation of spectrum for mobile television are of crucial importance – this issue needs to be addressed urgently in order to enable the launch of services as soon as possible.

REFERENCES

[1]   NOKIA, *Bringing TV into Mobile Phones*, Forum Nokia's Mobile Application Summit, Singapore, 18 June 2004.
[2]   A. Boni, E. Launay, T. Mienville and P. Stuckmann, *Multimedia Broadcast Multicast Service – Technology Overview and Service Aspects,* France Telecom R&D, 2005.
[3]   Alcatel (Strategy Whitepaper), 'Multimedia Broadcast and Multicast Services in 3G Mobile Networks,' *Alcatel Telecommunications Review* – 4th Quarter 2003/1st Quarter 2004.
[4]   Y. K. Kim and R. Prasad, *4G Roadmap and Emerging Communication Technologies*, Artech House, 2006.
[5]   P. Zeng and L. M. Ni, *Smart Phone & Next Generation Mobile Computing*, Elsevier (Morgan Kaufmann Publishers), Amsterdam, 2006.
[6]   NOKIA Whitepaper, *IP Datacasting – Bringing TV into Mobile Phones*, 2004.
[7]   A. Kumar, *Mobile TV; DVB-H, DMB, 3G Systems and Rich Media Applications*, Focal Press, Amsterdam, 2007.
[8]   ITU-R, *Final Acts WARC-07, Geneva*, 2007.
[9]   Decision 676/2002/EC of the European Parliament and of the Council of 7 March 2002 on a regulatory framework for radio spectrum policy in the European Community (Radio Spectrum Decision) (OJ L108/1 dated 24 April 2002).
[10] European Commission (2006): 'Commission staff working document on the Review of the EU Regulatory Framework for electronic

communications networks and services {COM(2006) 334 final}.'
SEC(2006) 816. Brussels, 28 June 2006.

[11]   S. Ramos, A. Moral, A. Vergara and J. Pérez, 'Strategic Policy
       Options on Spectrum Management for the Development of Mobile
       TV Market in Europe,' *16th IST Mobile and Wireless Communications Summit*, Budapest, Hungary, 1–5 July 2007.

[12]   RSPG, Radio Spectrum Policy Group Opinion on the Introduction
       of Multimedia Services. RSPG06-143 Final. October 2006.

8

Trials

The idea of employing point-to-multipoint techniques for multi-media delivery seems appealing. However, the specifications and standards related to the different technologies are not enough to evaluate whether they are applicable in real life. To prove the theory, many trials of multicast technologies have been conducted all over the world. Several aspects, such as efficiency, reliability, quality and in-motion reception, have been tested. Going one step further, new, more efficient delivery systems enable new, data-rich services. This aspect also needs to be evaluated; thus, during the trials, users' attitudes towards particular services were examined as well. Good results in the technical tests as well as positive user feedback contributed to several commercial rollouts of multicast-based delivery systems. In this chapter selected technical aspects of these trials and examples of commercial implementations will be briefly described, while the next chapter focuses on the user feedback. As we believe that DVB-H-based IP Datacast and MBMS are the most appropriate solutions for multicast delivery to mobile terminals, in this chapter we will focus on these two. During research, we found the results of MediaFLO tests interesting as well; thus, we will also cover them briefly.

As we know, IPDC and MediaFLO represent a different approach than MBMS. At first they may seem more attractive. However, a dedicated network separated from the existing cellular infrastructure needs to be built in order to provide the services. Major players invested a lot of money in developing and deploying packet-switched, 3G networks worldwide and they would rather see new services being

Multimedia Broadcasting and Multicasting in Mobile Networks
G. Iwacz, A. Jajszczyk and M. Zajączkowski
© 2008 John Wiley & Sons, Ltd

deployed on top of it. This makes MBMS preferable to IPDC or MediaFLO.

To avoid confusion, one issue should be explained. A video streaming service has been available in mobile networks for years. Since the end of 2005 over 40 operators have been offering mobile TV over the UMTS network [1]. For instance, Vodafone and Orange launched this service in the United Kingdom. However, the service is delivered in a unicast manner and each user downloads data separately with an average rate of 100 kbit/s. This can lead to a situation where a relatively small group of users consumes all the capacity. This first unicast video streaming service is still very important, as it can provide great feedback and form a good starting point for the future multicast services.

8.1   DVB-H TRIALS

IP Datacast is based on the DVB-H technology; therefore, tests on it are not as crucial as tests on DVB-H itself. Thus, we decided to broaden the scope of this part and show the test results of other DVB-H-based solutions similar to IPDC [2].

All over the world various aspects of DVB-H-based technologies are being, or have been, tested in practice. This has helped to solve many existing problems and has proved that the technology is efficient for delivery of new, multimedia services. Importantly, several large companies, including Nokia, Motorola, Siemens, Samsung, Orange, Vodafone, O2, T-Mobile, ABC and Sky, were involved in these trials. This proves that DVB-H is worth considering as a medium for delivery of mobile TV.

After significant technical aspects were tested, the technology stepped into the commercial implementation phase. Some networks are already used commercially and some are ready for launch in the near future. Table 8.1 lists DVB-H-based trials and implementations, which will be discussed shortly. As the data for the table was compiled in March 2008, some information may no longer be up to date. For the most current data please refer to [2].

At this moment in time (March 2008), over 40 trials are finished and 17 others are in progress. Apart from this, there are over 12 operational, commercial networks, with the leading ones in Italy and Finland. The service is free-to-air in many cases (in Finland, Albania and India). This is a good way to examine the market and

Table 8.1 DVB-H-based trials (as of March 2008) [2]

	Full service launch	Trial service (X = on-going trial; O = completed or results available)
Albania		
DigitALB	Launched	
Australia		
Sydney		O
Austria		
Nationwide	2008	
Vienna/Salzburg		O
Belgium		
Ghent/Brussels/Mechelen (MADUF)		X
Brussels (RTBF)		X
Canada		
Toronto		X
Denmark		
Copenhagen		O
Finland		
Mobiili-TV	Launched	
Helsinki		O
France		
Metz		X
Paris (TDF)		O
Paris (Canalı)		O
Pau (DVB-SH)		O
Nationwide	2008	
Germany		
Berlin (bmco)		O
Berlin (T-Systems)		X
Erlangen		X
Nationwide	2008	
Hong Kong		
Hong Kong (PCCW)		O
Hungary		
Budapest		O
India		
Delhi (Doordarshan)	Launched	
Indonesia		
Global Mediacom/NSN	2008	
Jakarta		O
Ireland		
Dublin		O
Italy		
3 Italia	Launched	
TIM TV	Launched	
Vodafone	Launched	
Turin		O
Kenya		
DStv	Launched	

Table 8.1   (Continued)

	Full service launch	Trial service (X = on-going trial; O = completed or results available)
Latvia		
Riga		X
Libya		
Tripoli		X
Malaysia		
Kuala Lumpur		X
MiTV	Launched	
Namibia		
MultiChoice/MTN	Launched	
Netherlands		
Nationwide (KPN/Digitenne)	2008	
The Hague		O
Nigeria		
Details Nigeria/MTN	Launched	
Philippines		
Manila (Dream Mobile TV)		O
MyTV (Smart & MediaScape)	Launched	
Poland		
Nationwide		X
Warsaw (TP Emitel #1)		X
Warsaw (TP Emitel #2)		O
Portugal		
Lisbon (TVI & RETI)		O
Lisbon (SGC Telecom)		O
Qatar		
Doha		O
Russian Federation		
Kaliningrad		O
Moscow (Dominanta)	2008	
Moscow (DTB)		O
Sverdlovsk Oblast TV Mobile		O
Singapore		
Innoxius		X
TV2Go		X
South Africa		
Johannesburg/Pretoria/Soweto/ Capetown		X
Spain		
Barcelona/Madrid		O
Seville (Axion Technical Trial)		O
Seville/Valencia		O
Zaragoza/Gijón		O
Sweden		
Gothenburg/Stockholm (Teliasonera)		O
Stockholm (Teracom)		O
Stockholm (Viasat)		O

Switzerland		
Bern (Customer Acceptance)		O
Bern (Technical)		O
Swisscom (MoTV)	2008	
Taiwan		
Taichung City (ChungWha Wideband)		X
Taipei (Nokia)		O
Taipei (PTS Consortium)		O
Ukraine		
Kiev		O
United Arab Emirates		
Dubai		O
United Kingdom		
Cambridge		O
Oxford		O
Uruguay		
Montevideo (Ancel)		X
USA		
Las Vegas (Hiwire)		O
ICO mim (DVB-SH)		X
New York City (Modeo)		O
Pittsburgh (Modeo)		O
Vietnam		
VTC	Launched	

gain more user feedback, as a significantly larger number of users is interested in a free service. Initially, all trials were carried out in big cities, with the service being launched in less-populated areas in the later stages.

The year 2008 will bring another seven commercial rollouts, mostly in Europe. Sporting events are the spark in all cases, as in 2008 we have the Olympic Games in Beijing and the UEFA European Football Championships in Austria and Switzerland. A network in Germany is intended to be launched just before these two sporting events. The situation is similar to 2006, when the mobile TV service was rolled out in Italy before the FIFA Football World Cup. In the next chapter we are going to discuss how different sporting events suit mobile reception and what the characteristics of the mobile content should be.

A large number of successfully finished trials proves that the technology is mature. Unfortunately, legal issues slow down the service rollouts in countries like France and Austria. Additionally, all involved parties struggle to divide the revenue and copyright issues are also continually discussed. This causes significant delays in service launch. Moreover, the spectrum itself is one of the problems. In countries like Finland, Italy and the USA this is not an issue, as these countries have settled all the spectrum concerns. However, this can be a problem globally.

As mentioned previously, many tests on DVB-H-based technologies have been carried out. These have included general technical tests, from the basic ones (Warsaw) through high velocity reception (Toronto) and urban and indoor coverage (Turin), to complex tests involving interactivity with other networks (Helsinki, Turin). So far, all the tests have been completed successfully. Trials seem to verify the theory. Thanks to the peculiar nature of broadcast transmission, a small number of transmitters can provide coverage for a wide area. For example, two transmitters (20 and 50 W ERP), were used to cover the whole city of Berlin. As we know, new infrastructure is necessary to provide the services; however, its cost is relatively low, which makes the investments insignificant in comparison to the forecast revenue. Uplink communication, using GPRS connections, and interactivity, e.g., through SMS, have also been tested. Both of these approaches seem to work fine. More detailed information about other trials can be found in [2].

The most significant services provided thanks to DVB-H are based on audio/video streaming. Thus, during the trials, services like television, audio/video transmission from certain events and radio were mainly evaluated. The H.263 compression format was used in the early stage trials. For the later ones, its new version, denoted H.264, was chosen. During the complex trials, where customer feedback was the main deliverable, a whole set of services which could be available for commercial use in future was available. For example, approximately 40 services, including TV, interactive TV, radio and various data services, were available during the Berlin trial. According to research by the Elisa Corporation (http://www.elisa.com), one of the participants in the Helsinki trial, there is a need to offer short clips during the day, since participants are mainly using the service for short periods.

One of the key factors leading to a successful technology deployment is related to the terminals. Without a small device with a relatively large screen, the described services would not be attractive enough. The early stage device was the Nokia 7710 terminal with a custom DVB-H receiver (Figure 8.1). The terminal is only available commercially without the DVB-H receiver.

Not only mobile phones were used in the tests; the services were tested on other devices as well. For example, PDAs with an

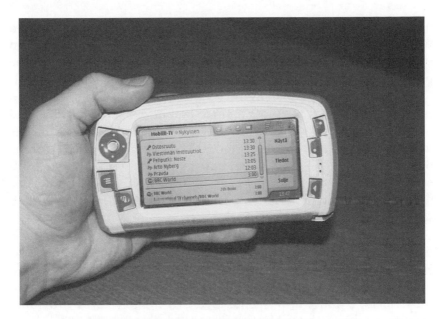

Figure 8.1 Nokia 7710 with DVB-H receiver (reproduced by permission of © 2008 Nokia Corporation and © 2008 BBC)

external DVB-H receiver were used during the tests by VTT Technical Research Centre of Finland. During our visit to the Elisa Corporation in 2006, we tested the TV service using the Nokia 7710 terminal. Video and audio quality was excellent and the compression was practically imperceptible. The screen size and resolution enable one to watch a regular TV channel and to clearly see and be able to read the subtitles. Since then, many companies have equipped their new terminals with DVB-H receivers. Some of these are listed below:

- Nokia: N92, N77;
- Samsung: SGH-P910, SGH-P920, SGH-P930, SGH-P940, SGH-F510;
- LG: U900, KU950;
- Sony Ericsson: K850;
- Sagem: My Mobile TV.

To launch the service, a relevant billing system is also necessary. Therefore, some tests in this field were made. According to research made by the Elisa Corporation, a constant monthly fee-based system would work best. Tests made during other trials seem to confirm this conclusion. This issue has been covered in greater detail in the previous chapter.

Multicast-based mobile TV became available for the first time in Italy. As this is now the most mature and developed DVB-H-based network in the world, we will include more details concerning its implementation. In Italy, the mobile TV service is provided by three operators. One of them, 3 Italia, has its own network of over 1000 radio transmitters, with power ranging from 5 W up to 2.5 kW. The network uses bandwidth ranging from 474 to 746 MHz. As a coding scheme, H.264/AAC+ was chosen.

The service was launched in April 2006 but the TV channels only became available in June 2006. Currently, the network covers 85% of the country's area, meaning that the service is available to around 48 million Italians. In May 2007 the service had 600,000 subscribers. 3 Italia now spends over 10 million euros providing content to its mobile TV service called 'Walk TV'. The company believes that having control over the whole service value chain, from the backbone network to content delivery, is the key to providing the best services. When we move to the business case, two different scenarios have been applied. These are Pay-TV bundled with voice and data transmission and prepaid access.

Another company with its own DVB-H infrastructure is Mediaset. It cost 250 million euros to build the network. At the moment, Mediaset sells off 25% of its network capacity to Vodafone and another 25% to Telecom Italia. Vodafone and Telecom Italia actually cooperate, thus we have three players on the Italian mobile TV market [3].

To better understand the technology, we will present some basic information about the infrastructure used during the Helsinki trial in 2005. Three transmitters along with three repeaters and some gap fillers were used. This was enough to provide good reception in the whole city of Helsinki, even indoors. Reception inside buildings with glass facades appeared to be a problem, though. The transmission rate of 270 kbit/s per stream was the basis for audio/video streaming services. The H.263 compression standard was employed. As for the frequency, an 8 MHz channel at the frequency of 610 MHz was used. Moreover, IPsec was responsible for security and a GPRS connection was used as an uplink channel.

8.2 MBMS TRIALS

As already mentioned, MBMS is a technology deployed using the existing 3G networks. Because of this, it is not necessary to test all aspects of MBMS. Thus, in comparison to DVB-H-based technologies, a limited number of tests have been carried out.

At present (March 2008) there is not a single commercially running MBMS implementation, although various tests have been conducted all over the world. The first one, led by Ericsson, took place in Stockholm in April 2005 and finished with success. The commercial rollout of the system is scheduled for 2008 and Ericsson's MBMS platform and terminals will be released to market at the same time.

Another significant trial was conducted by Orange, Vodafone, Telefonica and 3UK. IPWireless's solution, called TDtv, which is an extension of the 3GPP MBMS standard, was tested [4]. Even though the technology offers some enhancements when compared to MBMS, they are still pretty similar. TDtv uses the universal unpaired 3G spectrum bands of 1900 MHz and 2010 MHz. Other frequencies, including the 2.5 GHz band, will also be supported in future. The trial was announced in October 2006 and finished at the beginning of 2007. It took place in Bristol, United Kingdom. Crucial information concerning this trial is listed below [5]:

- Thanks to the applied enhancements, the number of high quality (300 kbit/s) channels delivered using 5 MHz bandwidth was up to 11. This could be increased to as many as 14 with some further upgrades. This number doubles when the 10 MHz bandwidth is available.
- The coverage was comparable to WCDMA. Interestingly, it could be achieved with approximately 35% of the transmitters. Again, this was possible thanks to some technologies enhancing TDtv performance.
- A large area of Bristol was covered with 12 macro-cell sites.
- The service was available during 99.999% of the trial time, making it very reliable.
- Reception in movement was consistent. For example, tests were made while traveling by train.
- The tested handset was able to operate in both WCDMA and TDtv modes simultaneously.

As we know, mobile network operators spent a lot of money on the development and implementation of 3G networks. A great deal of money was also spent on spectrum licenses, mainly in Europe. Thus, the operators are not keen on investing in other, competitive technologies. They would rather enhance the existing UMTS networks in order to provide a mobile TV service. For this reason we may expect pressure from mobile network operators to enforce 3G-based mobile TV rather than DVB-H-based solutions or MediaFLO. Moreover, launching a new service over 3G networks would give full control to 3G operators. They would not need to share revenue with the broadcasters. Only content would be an issue here. The MBMS implementation is easy and its costs are relatively low. Moreover, the revenue coming from new, multimedia, MBMS-based services would prove to the investors that it was a good idea to develop and deploy UMTS networks.

8.3   MEDIAFLO TRIALS

We believe that MediaFLO is the best SFN (Single Frequency Network) alternative to DVB-H-based solutions. Thus, MediaFLO trials are also covered here. According to [6], the first trial was conducted during the summer of 2006. During this trial, based in Cambridge, UK, Qualcomm was assisted by British Sky Broadcasting Limited (BSkyB). During this two-month period, 11 BSkyB channels were available to a relatively small number of terminals provided by Qualcomm. Issues including network acquisition, channel-switching times, layered modulation and video codec performance as well as total throughput were tested. The main objective of these tests was to prove the performance in a mixed-field test environment.

The next significant trial was also conducted in the UK during the winter of 2006 in Manchester. The goal here was similar to the Cambridge trial. Moreover, a comparison between the performance of FLO and DVB-H was made. The information obtained during the trials has been gathered below:

- General FLO performance was confirmed: it is able to provide 20 QVGA video channels with stereo audio in the 5 MHz bandwidth. Before the trials, this number of channels was estimated to be available using the 6 MHz bandwidth, which means a 20% improvement over the theoretical results.

- Users were pleased with the quality of 25 frames per second, 240 kbit/s audio/video streams.
- Access time to the channel guide was approximately 2 seconds, while the physical layer was available after about 1.5 seconds and the waiting time for the audio/video stream was around 2.1 seconds.
- The physical layer performance was better than predicted.
- MediaFLO flexibility allows a trade-off of approximately half the channels to double the coverage.

In 2007, additional trials were carried out in Taipei, Taiwan and in Malaysia. The first one was conducted with partners such as China Network Systems and Taiwan Television Enterprise Ltd. The Malaysian tests were made in cooperation with Maxis Communications Berhad and ASTRO All Asia Networks plc.

Nationwide MediaFLO deployment is also being considered in Japan. Moreover, Verizon Wireless is considering commercial rollout of the service in the United States

REFERENCES

[1] Ericsson (press information), *Bringing mobile TV to the masses*, February 2006.
[2] DVB Project, *DVB-H Services*, http://www.dvb-h.org/services.htm, 22 August 2006.
[3] Lehman Brothers, *Mobile Television* , Global Equity Research, August 2006.
[4] IPWireless, Inc. home page, http://www.ipwireless.com.
[5] IPWireless, *Vodafone, Telefónica, Orange and 3UK Report Successful Results from TDtv Trial with IPWireless and MobiTV*, http://www.ipwireless.com/solutions/ mobile_tv.html, 14 November 2007.
[6] MediaFLO home page, http://www.qualcomm.com/mediaflo/index.shtml, 14 November 2007.

9

User Feedback

In this book we describe multicast as a technology predestined to provide new, high quality multimedia services. We have focused on various technical aspects, with some implementation issues also covered. Still, the introduction of a very promising service, powered by the newest technologies, without customer interest may result in a market failure. It is customers' attitude towards the service that can cause its success or failure. In other words, customer feedback is an important issue to consider and cannot be neglected. Therefore, in this chapter we discuss the feedback from various mobile television trials.

Multicast is the delivery technique that enables resource savings in the backbone network as well as in the last mile link. Therefore, more bandwidth is available for the customer. Furthermore, in the IPDC case, deployment of SFN (Single Frequency Network) increases the bandwidth and operators benefit. A user still benefits indirectly since, thanks to a higher bandwidth, new services are available. As we have already mentioned, mobile television is the most spectacular and significant service enabled by multicast. Thus, this chapter is limited to topics concerning mobile television.

First of all, the general user attitude will be described. Some threats, as well as potential reasons for service failure, will be discussed. Next, we will cover some business-oriented issues, including users' attitude towards mobile TV as a paid service, users' opinions and future predictions. Following this, to better understand the customers' point of view, some usage scenarios will be introduced.

Multimedia Broadcasting and Multicasting in Mobile Networks
G. Iwacz, A. Jajszczyk and M. Zajączkowski
© 2008 John Wiley & Sons, Ltd

Finally, we will take a look at the future of mobile TV and discuss some of its social aspects.

9.1   INTEREST

Generally, the idea of multicast-based multimedia delivery seems appropriate. Professionals agree that it would increase network performance, providing new, rich multimedia services. From the technical point of view, it would be a major step forward. However, when it comes to commercial issues, things get more complicated. Many people do not believe that mobile TV will be a success and accordingly question the idea of investing in this new technology, being sure of witnessing a spectacular failure. Their arguments include such potential drawbacks as low usage comfort and small screen size. On the other hand, a lot of people believe the service will be a great financial success and are convinced that it will become a *cash cow* in the near future. The whole dispute between service enthusiasts and their opponents is meaningless when we take a look at opinion poll results. Users participating in various mobile TV trials all over the world were asked about their attitude towards the service. Most of the respondents were more than satisfied. Figure 9.1 shows some of the results.

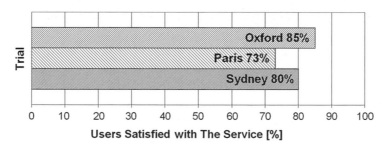

Figure 9.1   Percentage of users satisfied with the service

In Spain, users were asked if they would recommend the service. In Seville and Valencia 80% said 'Yes', while in Barcelona and Madrid it was 75% [1].

In the United States, Crown Castles' subsidiary, Modeo, launched mobile TV as a beta service in New York City. The company, however, withdrew the idea of commercial launch and leased the spectrum reserved for the service. Still, over 130 'friendly users' gave great feedback. Almost every respondent was satisfied (99%) or very satisfied (64%) with the picture quality. Service availability was highly rated as well. Around 87% of respondents were satisfied and 37% were very satisfied. Moreover, the users were very positive about the service in general. Questioned about having a live TV and radio service on their mobile phone, 98% were positive and 75% very positive [1].

To sum up, the majority of respondents were positive about the service. Similar polls have been carried out all over the world and we can clearly see that the results are not based on some specific cultural background.

9.2 THREATS

Since not all the respondents were so satisfied, the potential threats should be discussed. Actually, there is no relevant data concerning the reasons for dissatisfaction. However, we presume that these may be related to:

- low service quality;
- insufficient content scope;
- low usage comfort;
- high cost.

In the following sections we will address these issues. Starting with the audio/video transmission quality, we can clearly say that it is very good, and the minor distortions that can occur due to the compression are insignificant and hard to observe at all. Next, we should consider the size of the screen in mobile terminals as a potential problem source. For example, the Nokia N92 is equipped with a 2.8' screen (320×240 pixels, up to 16 million colors). In some situations this may just not be enough. However, many programs like news, weather forecasts, cartoons and sports events can be followed with appropriate comfort. Moreover, the screen is large enough that the user is able to read subtitles without effort. According to research undertaken by us, only 17% of the respondents pointed to low video quality as a major problem. A survey made by Modeo clarified that this should not be a reason for service failure. Almost every survey participant claimed to be satisfied with the picture quality.

The proposed content scope may be another reason for users' dissatisfaction. Programs that are available at this moment are suited to terrestrial television. Thus, some of the program types may seem unattractive when considering mobile reception. On the other hand, in France for example, 80% of trial users were satisfied with the proposed content. However, one way or another, program length and high quality video requirements may be a problem in this situation. But this can be easily solved. Short programs with low bandwidth requirements can be chosen as the mobile TV content. Moreover, programs specifically for mobile reception may be produced at a relatively low cost. Thus, the unsuitable content problem seems to be insignificant. However, we will still discuss this issue further in this chapter.

As we know, people are used to watching TV in the traditional way; that is, during their free time while sitting on a comfortable couch at home. They can feel uncomfortable while watching TV on the move, in public places like buses or trams. Thus, the lack of comfort can be treated as one of the threats. These are, however, not related to the signal quality, as there are no problems with reception during movement. A series of tests conducted in Canada showed that undistorted transmission is possible while traveling at a speed of about 120 km/h on a highway and at a speed of about 60 km/h in a city area.

Another issue is related to the complexity of using the service. In one of the trials in Seville and Valencia in Spain, eight out of ten trial participants declared that the service was easy to use, which was achieved thanks to the Electronic Service Guide (ESG).

During tests in Oxford, UK, the main satisfaction drivers were: good audio and video quality, the ESG and a large variety of channels. Figure 9.2 shows these main success factors [2].

Figure 9.2   Mobile TV success factors [2]

9.3 BUSINESS ISSUES

The majority of users originating from various world regions were satisfied with the service. However, their satisfaction does not guarantee mobile TV success. It still needs to generate revenue to be called successful. In this case most of the money would come from charging the user (the rest would come from advertisers). Taking this into consideration, the key question here is how many potential customers would pay to watch television on their mobile terminals? Figure 9.3 shows the answer to this question.

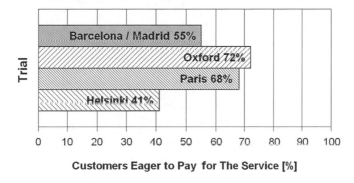

Figure 9.3 Percentage of customers eager to pay for the service

In all agglomerations, the percentage of users eager to pay is at a relatively high level. For example, in Oxford, almost three quarters of users would pay for the service. Unfortunately, the results depend on the region.

A large number of customers still does not guarantee a decent profitability level. Also, the monthly fee needs to be considered here. In Helsinki, the trial participants declared that they would pay between 5 and 10 euros per month. In Paris it was 7 or more, and in Barcelona/Madrid 5 euros.

As unicast- and multicast-based services do not differ much from the user point of view, we will briefly present the feedback given by the users of the Ericsson unicast-based mobile TV service [3]. First of all, the main conclusion is that there is a need for such a service. A lot of people are interested. Moreover, customers are eager to pay a monthly fee of 10 to 15 euros for unlimited access to a multichannel service.

Concluding, users are eager to pay for the service. Such a level of monthly income would make the service quite profitable; however, this again depends on the region.

9.4 USAGE SCHEMES

The place and method of usage are extremely important for the network operators. Indoor or outdoor as well as static or in movement reception are the major issues here. Participants in the trial in Paris were asked where they would mainly use the service. Figure 9.4 shows how they answered.

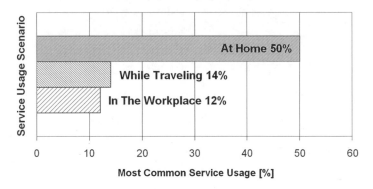

Figure 9.4   Service usage scenarios [1]

We need to keep in mind that during the pilot, all the subway lines were out of the coverage range. If the service was also available there, this would surely increase the percentage of use while traveling. Moreover, according to the research made in Oxford, users at an initial stage preferred to use the service at home, while in the later stages, commuting was the most common background. This is surely related to usage comfort. In the early stages we do not know the service and thus do not feel confident and comfortable using it. In this situation each of us would first try it at home rather than in a crowded place where our attention is distracted. 37% of all usage during the Oxford trial happened while traveling and it was the most common situation [1]. In conclusion, much attention must be paid to indoor coverage as well as to reception while on the move.

According to research, the most popular usage scenarios are filling short time gaps, watching during waiting and staying up to date. Daytime usage is strictly related to the place and situation. Thus, the peak usage time was in the morning and evening (the commuting period). This was followed by some short time periods during the day (break at work, etc.).

So far we have covered issues that are relevant to network operators. Now we will focus on the service itself. Most of the users were satisfied with the content proposed. However, all of the channels were regular, known terrestrial television channels, not suited to mobile reception at all. So what enhancements should be introduced to make the content more 'mobile'? The key factors are the program length and users' preferences. Figures 9.5 and 9.6 illustrate the average usage time [1].

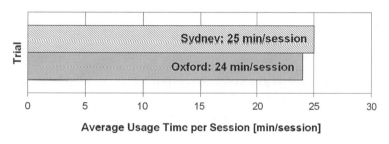

Figure 9.5   Average service usage time per session [1]

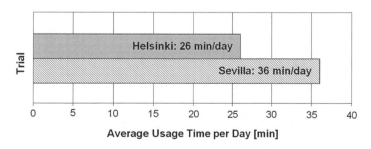

Figure 9.6   Average service usage time per day [1]

The results from the Modeo trial in the United States are very similar. The average usage time was 15 minutes per day. Viewing sessions lasted for 30–35 minutes and the usage rose during weekends.

In addition, 52% of trial users claimed to watch more television as a result of having a mobile terminal. This means that mobile handsets are used in situations where a traditional TV set is unavailable. Mobile television will not replace the traditional couch TV, it will only extend it for some content and for situations where we are out of our homes. Scenarios like queuing or traveling are relevant examples. These are situations where the user is bored, thus mobile TV is simply a good way to kill the boredom.

As we have mentioned before, there is a relationship between the usage time and place. Moreover, a relationship between the place and usage length also exists. For example, typical usage scenarios during one of the trials were:

- **Short waiting periods:** less than 5 minutes, in the waiting room or while waiting for public transportation.
- **Medium periods:** up to 30 minutes in a car or bus.
- **Long periods:** over 30 minutes, usually indoors (home, restaurant).

Next we will list some common program types from the mobile TV user perspective [2]:

- **News:** video is rather static so it is easy to follow, it is available 24 hours per day and it usually does not matter at which part of the program the user joins. Moreover, it becomes extremely important when some extraordinary event happens.
- **Sport:** easy to follow in every situation.
- **Series and entertainment:** well-known characters and close zooms make it easy to follow. There is no need to follow the plot. Moreover, the length is close to the average usage time.
- **Music:** easy to watch and listen to; rapidly changing content makes it easy to join and leave at any time. Even short usage periods keep the user entertained.
- **Movies:** can be a substitute for regular television when we have to go out and do not want to miss the ending of the movie or there is no TV set.

This short list shows the most significant features of mobile-suited content. It should be as long as the average usage time, easy to follow and the action should be rather static. Taking this into consideration, news is the best content type in this situation, followed by series, sport and music channels. Sports events play a particular role in this field. Some of them can dominate viewing. This was the case with the football championships which were the spark to launch the service in Italy.

So far we have not mentioned another very interesting type of content, namely *podcasts*. Originally, this term was related to short audition-like audio content. Over time, podcasts evolved and now may be regarded as rich audio–video content as well. For example, we have *photocasts*, which are similar to slideshows with background audio streams, and *screencasts*, which are recorded computer screen actions with comments. The purpose of podcasts is mainly to entertain. However, quite often they bring some knowledge to the listener. Screencasts are a relevant example of podcasts that educate. To conclude, relatively short podcasts with nonabsorbing video sequences can be a very popular content type for mobile terminals.

In this section we have discussed the most suitable content types; however, we considered only existing types of program. At this point we know how mobile users behave and what they need in the mobile context. Thanks to this, content providers may create new, mobile-dedicated content by re-editing existing programs or simply by making new ones. We will discuss this issue later on in the context of the next generation mobile TV.

9.5 THE USER

We should be aware of one significant peculiarity while discussing program type preferences. This concerns the definition of *fun* in relation to entertainment. Every type of program generates a different type of fun. Furthermore, for some people fun may mean something completely different than for others. We can distinguish two main types of entertainment. The first one is active and exciting. Its main purpose is to kill boredom. This type is suitable for young people searching for stimulation through entertainment. The other type, in contrast to the first, is rather passive and calming. This is perfect for people looking for relaxation or a means of escape from everyday stress, as well as for older people. Figure 9.7 shows the relationship between the type of fun and the customer's mood. It is good to bear this in mind while considering the offered content.

We have showed that mobile TV as a paid service is bound to become popular. So far, however, we have not discussed how quickly

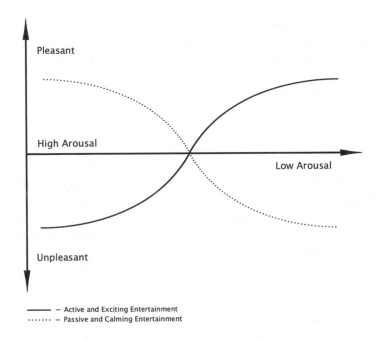

Figure 9.7   Relationship between people's mood and the preferred type of entertainment [4]

it will gain popularity. According to [2] users can be divided into five groups:

- **Innovators:** people who would purchase the service after launch.
- **Early adopters:** they would purchase a subscription while buying a new terminal.
- **Early majority:** these people declared that they would buy it when it became more popular.
- **Late majority:** they declared they may purchase it in the future.
- **Laggards/rejecters:** they would never buy a mobile TV service.

Figure 9.8 shows how big these groups are. Of course the two groups that will lead the sales of mobile TV in the early stages are 'Innovators' and 'Early adopters'.

The service may have some problems at takeoff, as 'Innovators' and 'Early adopters' are two relatively small groups. Still, the interest expressed by these groups may help to make the service more popular. After gaining a critical number of users, the 'snowball effect' should cause further growth.

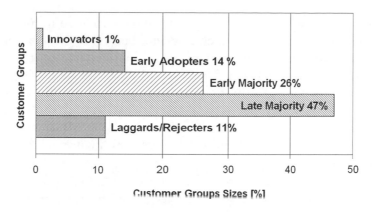

Figure 9.8   Division of users with respect to adoption of new services [2]

9.6   COMPARISON OF SERVICES

To get a better picture of mobile TV and its potential, we are going to compare it with more mature services in various contexts. The crucial issue to consider while evaluating the success or failure of services is the potential interest rate. According to a Siemens survey [5] conducted in November 2005 among 5300 subscribers from eight countries, mobile TV is definitively attractive, with a relatively high level of interest. The results of the survey are shown in Figure 9.9.

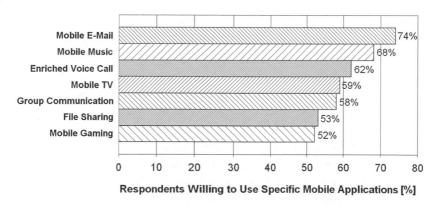

Figure 9.9   Interest rates for various mobile TV services [5]

As we can see, email applications are the most popular. 74% of respondents claimed that they were willing to use them. In the survey, mobile TV placed 4th with 59%, but we have to keep in mind that many users have never used such a service before. In this context the result is satisfying, as we believe it would be better if more people were familiar with mobile TV.

Now let us compare the services in the context of the monthly downlink data usage per typical user. This should show us the amount of resources consumed by the services, thus illustrating for which of the services the bandwidth is crucial. Figure 9.10 presents this comparison.

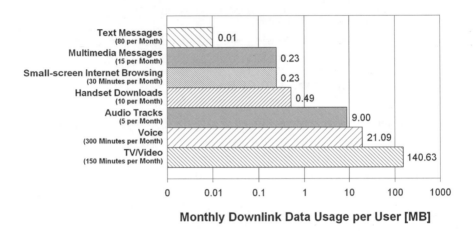

Figure 9.10   Downlink data usage for various services [6]

Out of the considered services, TV/video is the most bandwidth consuming. Moreover, one item is downloaded or streamed multiple times by different users. These two facts lead to the conclusion that multicast-based technologies are most suitable for TV/video delivery.

Next, changing the point of view, we shall compare mobile TV with regular television and radio. The question is whether it is possible for mobile TV to provide a good substitute for traditional television or radio and, if so, in what situations and for what reasons. Figure 9.11 may shed light on this question.

The key to answering this question is the fact that we usually have our mobile terminal with us all the time, for example while traveling, queuing or during some other idle time. In this context it is a perfect solution for 'killing' boredom. People would less likely use it for learning or relaxing. This is because of the usage context, as we usually relax or learn at home where traditional TV is available.

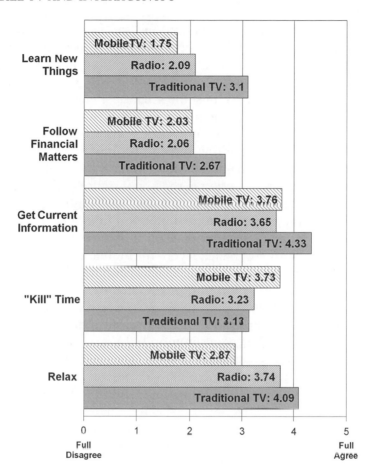

Figure 9.11 Comparison of mobile TV, traditional TV and radio in various contexts [7]

9.7 MOBILE TV AND INTERACTIVITY

Not so long ago, Ericsson, in cooperation with the Norwegian Broadcasting Corporation (NRK), conducted a study that provided some interesting results. It turned out that mobile TV services which were interactive were chosen twice as often as the regular ones. This may be a significant hint to the operators. For this reason, we shall discuss this issue in more detail.

Mobile TV is based on high quality audio/video streams for mobile terminals but it is not just a mobile version of the terrestrial service. The difference between these two is not only the screen size or the available content. The usage context and the fact that mobile TV is accessed using a terminal that provides peer-to-peer connectivity change it significantly. Terminal screen limitations and usage scenarios decrease the watching comfort, thus it will not be used as a substitute for traditional TV in some scenarios. For example, let us now consider a situation where a new action movie is available. It is far better to watch this on a wide screen, surrounded by a set of speakers than on the tiny screen of a mobile terminal using earphones. On the other hand, mobile terminals have been designed for peer-to-peer communication in the first instance and incorporate functionalities that provide easy-to-use and relatively cheap communication. All of these may be used in addition to mobile TV services but, additionally, all these communication features have the potential to shift mobile TV to a higher level – the mobile phone may evolve into an interactive, social and mobile television terminal. However, the evolution of mobile TV is not only related to its interactive capabilities. The content provided to the mobile terminals is key to its success as well. In Figure 9.12 we can see how these two factors enable a shift to the 3rd generation mobile TV service.

Re-broadcasting of programs available for terrestrial receivers was the first approach to providing mobile TV content. It is quite obvious that the mobile context and terminal capabilities may make traditional content unattractive. Short, visually unabsorbing content is far better suited, meaning there is a need to re-edit the traditional content or even make content for mobile terminals exclusively.

Providing full interactivity and making a mobile TV social is a more complex issue, thus we will cover this topic in more detail. The first problem that needs to be solved in order to provide peer-to-peer connectivity is peer discovery. While watching the news or an episode of our favorite comedy series, we need to be notified who else is watching, indicating to whom we can send a message. Moreover, the potential peers should be grouped, sorted or marked in such a way that we can easily recognize our friend in the group of all viewers or at least peers of a similar profile.

Another significant issue here is the interaction itself. It can be achieved in many different ways, including chat messages, instant messaging or even using a web forum or a blog. Attracting attention is something that must be considered when choosing and implementing the interaction method. While using the service in the mobile context, our attention is limited and additional activity makes the situation even worse; for example, using a standard numeric

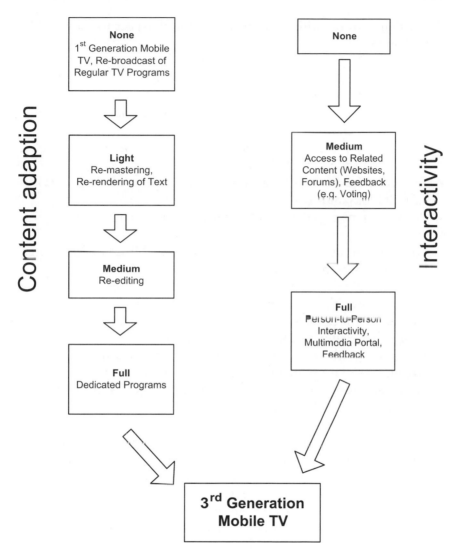

Figure 9.12   Mobile TV evolution [8]

keyboard for entering long messages while watching a video may be really distracting. The interaction type and integration are key issues here. Social features must be easy to use and have very low distraction properties. Otherwise, it may affect not only the additional services but mobile TV itself. For example, pop-ups with messages are definitely a bad idea, while background message notifications seem to be a far better solution. Many different approaches in many different dimensions can be utilized to push the social aspect to mobile TV, including [8]:

- **One-to-one:** peers appear and communicate in a one-to-one manner (e.g., instant messaging).
- **One-to-many:** all the peers using the service 'meet' in one spot (e.g., group chats).
- **Synchronous/real-time:** messages are delivered immediately (e.g., instant messaging, text chats).
- **Asynchronous:** content is accessible asynchronously (e.g., service-related blogs and forums).
- **Push:** content is pushed to the terminal (e.g., chat, instant messages).
- **Pull:** the user must download the content by himself/herself (e.g., by visiting service-related websites).
- **Low bandwidth:** simple services like basic text messaging.
- **High bandwidth:** complex, resource-consuming services.
- **Verbal:** text messages for example.
- **Nonverbal:** using symbols or emoticons.
- **Integrated with TV:** content related to the main audio/video streaming service (e.g., dedicated web pages or chats).
- **Separated from TV:** services not related to the TV content (e.g., separate chat room or instant messaging).

In our opinion, real-time, pushed and integrated services are the most desirable, while only almost real-time interaction can build the impression of a social service. Phatic messages like emoticons are very important as they are easy to use. On the other hand, relevant content available on web pages or blogs and forums may gather users interested in a particular service, and as the outcome build a society in the longer term.

As we are aware, multicast itself provides the downlink only. Thus, implementing interactivity without any other supporting technology is impossible. Fortunately, existing cellular networks can help us to solve this problem. UMTS offers us a high-speed uplink channel, while data transmission over GSM networks is slower, but still fast enough to provide high quality interactive services. Figure 9.13 helps us understand what such a hybrid architecture would look like.

To conclude, dedicated content and interaction will move mobile TV to a higher level, as peer-to-peer communication will push the service into a social context. Moreover, the social aspect of the service

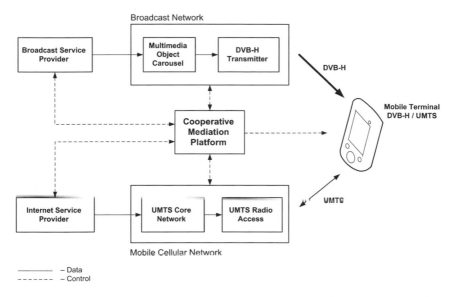

Figure 9.13 Hybrid network architecture enabling interactive services for mobile TV [9]

may become more significant in some situations, as it may last longer than the main audio/video streaming service itself. An example of such a scenario would be chatting or visiting service-related websites like blogs or forums. Finally, while mobile phones are usually considered as potential mobile TV receivers, implementing interactivity will not be a problem.

9.8 SUMMARY

At this moment we know the potential users, we know what they would like to watch and for how long. These are the key issues that need to be considered by the content and service providers. In addition to this, we know where, when and how the service would be used, which is extremely important for the network operators. We also know how interactivity and the social aspect would change the service. Finally, we know how many potential customers the service would attract and how much they would be willing to pay for it. And this is extremely important from the business point of view. However, in this case satisfying survey results are not enough, as it is a far cry from good feedback results to service success.

REFERENCES

[1] DVB Project, *DVB-H Services*, http://www.dvb-h.org/services.htm, 22 August 2006.
[2] J. Mäki, *Finnish Mobile TV Pilot*, Research International, Finland 2005.
[3] Ericsson (press information), *Bringing mobile TV to the masses*, February 2006.
[4] M. J. Apter, *Reversal Theory: Motivation, Emotion, and Personality*, Routledge, London, 1989.
[5] Lehman Brothers, *Mobile Television*, Global Equity Research, August 2006.
[6] L. D. Paulson, 'TV Comes to the Mobile Phone,' *IEEE Computer*, **39**(4), April 2006.
[7] C. Carlsson and P. Walden, 'Mobile TV – To Live or Die by Content,' *Proceedings of the 40th Hawaii International Conference on Systems Sciences*, IEEE Computer Society, 2007.
[8] R. Schatz, S. Wagner, S. Egger and N. Jordan, 'Mobile TV Becomes Social – Integrating Content with Communications,' *Proceedings of the ITI 2007 29th International Conference on Information Technology Interfaces*, Cavtat/Dubrovnik, Croatia, 25–28 June 2007.
[9] R. Schatz, N. Jordan and S. Wagner, 'Beyond Broadcast – A Hybrid Testbed for Mobile TV 2.0 Services,' *Proceedings of the Sixth International Conference on Networking ICN'07*, Sainte-Luce, Martinique, 22–28 April 2007.

10

Conclusion

If we take a closer look at the IT and telecommunications market, we will see that new innovative technologies are constantly emerging at an increasing pace and the existing ones are undergoing a process of constant evolution. In addition, the consumers are expecting more and more from their mobile terminals as well as from content providers. Offering plain old voice or text services is just not enough these days to satisfy a demanding end-user. Current and future services should be, one might say, revolutionary, meaning multimedia, innovative, appealing to users and, really importantly, interactive.

As far as we are concerned, the technologies based on the *multicast* concept have been proven feasible as a means of providing true multimedia services, in particular mobile television. The solutions on which we have focused – *Internet Protocol Datacasting* (IPDC) and *Multimedia Broadcast/Multicast Service* (MBMS) – both enable delivery of a high-quality television service, but at the same time also have their limitations. Although each of these can be used for providing a television service to mobile terminals, it is still apparent that IPDC and MBMS are better suited for different applications. There are, of course, several alternatives, described in detail in Chapter 5, but we consider IPDC and MBMS as the leading broadcast contenders.

IPDC, based on the DVB-H technology, is predestined to serve large groups of users (at least several consumers accessing the same content) within a specified coverage area, enabling data rates up to 22 Mbit/s. The consumers are offered a wide set of high quality TV channels (usually around 50) and additional services, together with interactive ones after integration with cellular networks. As the data is transmitted over a digital terrestrial broadcast network, a new dedicated infrastructure needs to be built and maintained, which obviously implies additional investment costs (as it turns out, the costs are not that high after all). It also constrains offering services to areas where the IPDC (DVB-H) networks have been deployed (usually densely populated metropolitan areas). On the other hand, as a separate infrastructure is used, the problem of congestion in cellular networks is avoided.

MBMS starts being effective when as few as only two users are accessing the same content. The solution uses the cellular network infrastructure already in place. This maximally reduces the deployment costs, as only one additional entity (the BM-SC) and some minor changes to the existing equipment are needed. In particular, some of the currently offered mobile terminals require only a minor software upgrade to be able to access the service.

However, while considering existing cellular networks, the congestion problem has to be faced. MBMS solves it partially, since its main aim is to avoid data duplication in the core as well as in the access network, but still the issue of excessive traffic must be taken into consideration. One advantage of the MBMS solution is that the offered content can be more personalized, while in some cases it can be addressed to a group of only two users. Additionally, the service can be offered in any place across the country, as right now cellular networks are present practically everywhere. Also, interactivity is easily assured, since the data link in cellular networks is bidirectional.

Regardless of all the advantages of MBMS, we have to be aware that it might not be an optimal solution for providing long-duration broadcasting streams like television programs. When we are dealing with heavy-duty streaming for wide audiences over a large geographical area, solutions such as IPDC are more suitable. Thus, MBMS can be treated as a complement to dedicated broadcast networks by delivering local content to a limited audience over smaller coverage areas. From here there is only one more step to the convergence of systems, where IPDC and MBMS, along with other access networks (DMB, WiFi, WiMAX, WiBro, Bluetooth, etc.), will form a monolithic arrangement of systems, a network of networks, providing a seamless service while the user is mobile. The technologies will complement each other in an optimal way to satisfy the end-user's needs.

It is worth mentioning that the deployment of the described systems and, following that, the introduction of new services available thanks to them, will be beneficial not only to the users and the owners of the networks (in most cases those are the existing cellular network operators), but also to all the other parties involved. Content providers may gain a new distribution channel offering existing or specially prepared content. Moreover, completely new audiences may be reached, namely people that are not present at home in front of their TV sets. All of this with only limited additional costs. As for the cellular network operators, they will be able to offer customers a completely new and desirable service. Finally, their revenues will grow thanks to the increased traffic in the network via the uplink channel.

Last but certainly not least, a couple of words about the customers' attitude towards mobile television. Looking at the users' feedback described in Chapter 9 it becomes apparent that there is a strong need for such a service as mobile television, since, for example, around 75% of those questioned in Madrid would recommend the service and in New York 98% were positive or very positive about having a live TV and radio service on their mobile phone. Moreover, typically over 50% of the respondents in various European cities would be eager to pay for watching television on their mobile terminals. In Oxford, only 25% stated that they would not pay for it. Unfortunately, the service is still not available in many countries worldwide; however, the presented results may provide a cue for the cellular network operators and other parties considering service launch. Especially given that the initial deployment cost is not that high and the possible revenues are outstanding. And if the basic service is enhanced by interactivity aspects using the existing cellular networks, the revenues may be further increased thanks to additional data traffic in the network.

To summarize, in our opinion, solutions and services based on multicast technologies are bound to become more and more widely deployed while their supremacy over point-to-point delivery techniques is indisputable. We may even recognize IPDC and MBMS solutions as the driving force of mobile service development in the upcoming years. Special attention needs to be given to the mobile television service, as it has all it takes to become the next *killer application*.

Further Reading

[1] ETSI TR 102401 v1.1.1 (2005–05), *Digital Video Broadcasting (DVB): Transmission to Handheld Terminals (DVB-H), Validation Task Force Report.*

[2] IPWireless, *TDtv: The Mobile TV and Multimedia Solutions Designed for UMTS Operators*, http://www.ipwireless.com/solutions/mobile_tv.html, 14 November 2007.

[3] mobileTV news Web Portal, *Quaestor Conducts Study Exploring Mobile TV Use Amongst Children*, http://www.mobiletv-news.com/content/view/193/2, 11 July 2006.

[4] RFC 3170 – Informational (B. Quinn and K. Almeroth), *IP Multicast Applications: Challenges and Solutions*, September 2001.

[5] WiMAX Forum Whitepaper, 'WiMAX's Technology for LOS and NLOS Environment,' *The WiMAX Forum*, Hillsboro, OR, 2004.

Multimedia Broadcasting and Multicasting in Mobile Networks
G. Iwacz, A. Jajszczyk and M. Zajączkowski
© 2008 John Wiley & Sons, Ltd

Index

Bold numbers denote the key material on this subject

2G   49, 60
2.5G   2, 49, 60, 68
2k mode   30, 32, 37, 38
3G   23, 49, 50, 56, 60, 68, 69,
   109, 123, 124, 129, 133, 141,
   149, 150
3GPP   55, 60, 98, 149
4k mode   28, 31, 32, **37–8**
8k mode   30, 32, 37, 38

Access   5, 6, 14, 15, 18, 19,
   21, 23, 26, 31, 43, 49,
   50, 55, 59, 61, 65, 67, 68,
   73, 75, 82, 89, 90, 92, 109,
   111, 112, 115, 117–21, 124,
   127, 130–3, 137, 148,
   151, 157
   access control   14, 26, 74, 75
   access network   16, 19
   unauthorized access   3, 63
Advanced Encryption Standard
   (AES), see Encryption
Advanced Television Systems
   Committee (ATSC)   28
Application Data Table (ADT)
   36, 37
Association of Radio Industries
   and Businesses (ARIB)   88,
   89, 98
Asynchronous Layered Coding
   (ALC), see Coding

Authentication   14, 15, 50, 63,
   102, 106, 108, 109, 110
Authentication Header (AH)
   107
Authentication and Key
   Agreement (AKA)   63
   biometric authentication   113
   Keyed-Hashing for Message
   Authentication   110
Authorization   14, 18, 30,
   61, 63

Backbone   9, 14, 19, 148, 153
Background class   **64**, 65
Bandwidth   5, 9, 10, 12, 23, 26,
   29, 30, 31, 45, 49, 50, 55, 56,
   59, 65, 68, 71, 73, 76, 77,
   79, 86, 90, 92, 93, 108, 126,
   138, 148, 149, 150, 153, 156,
   164, 168
Basic pull model   **104**
Battery   21, 23, 26, 29, 30, 34, 37,
   74, 86, 113, 126
Bearer context   63, 64
Billing   14, 15, 17, 45, 50, 73,
   101, 117, 120, 122, 130,
   131, 147
Binary Format for Scenes
   (BIFS)   82
Bit interleaving, see Interleaving
Bluetooth   67, 172

Broadcast 3, 5, 6, 7, 8, 26, 27, 28,
    40, 43, 50, 51, 56–9, 61, 63,
    66, 67, 71, 72, 78, 86, 88, 97,
    101, 119, 121, 124, 146, 171
  broadcast network, see Network
  broadcast service 40, 43, 50,
    56, 57, 62
  free-to-air broadcast 121
Broadcast/Multicast Service Center
    (BM-SC) 56, 58, 61–4, 68,
    121, 172
Business 16, 77, 105, 112, 115,
    116, 117, 121, 128, 129, 130,
    132, 138, 148, 169
  business aspects 3, 24, 56
  business issues 153, **157–8**

Carousel **65–6**, 80
Carrier-to-noise (C/N) 31, 36
CDMA, see Code Division
    Multiple Access
Cell phone 1, 23, 89, 124, 126
Channel 18, 19, 24, 29, 30, 31,
    36, 38, 40, 43, 47–50, 57, 59,
    66, 73, 75, 76, 78, 79, 82, 84,
    86, 87, 88, 90, 92, 93, 98,
    105, 116, 117, 118, 130, 132,
    148–51, 156, 159, 160, 173
  interaction channel **48–51**
  main service channel (MSC) 84
  purchase channel 43
  return channel 8, 90, 120
  synchronization channel 84
  television (TV) channel 24, 43,
    65, 79, 90, 98, 128, 147,
    148, 159, 171, 172
  uplink channel, see Uplink
Charging 3, 15, 50, 57, 61,
    62, 66, 67, 117, 121,
    130–2, 157
Code Division Multiple Access
    (CDMA) 50, 133
  CDMA 2000 50

Wideband Code Division
    Multiple Access (WCDMA)
    50, 55, 57, 68, 133, 149
Coded Orthogonal Frequency
    Division Multiplexing
    (COFDM) 28, 29
Coding 22, 25, 28, 62, 73, 75, 78,
    81, 82, 84, 88, 89, 92, 98, 148
  Advanced Audio Coding (AAC)
    45, 82
  Advanced Video Coding (AVC)
    30, 45, 82
  Asynchronous Layered Coding
    (ALC) 28, 47, 48
  channel coding 82, 83, 84, 90,
    93, 94, 95
  convolutional coding 28, 84
  FEC coding 31
  source coding 81, 82, 89
Compression 30, 45, 82, 127,
    146, 147, 148, 155
  audio/video compression 24
  video compression 45
Confidentiality 106–9
Congestion 14, 172
  congestion control 15, 16, 48
Content 2, 3, 5, 6, 7, 14, 16, 18,
    25, 40, 42, 43, 45, 47–50, 56,
    61, 62, 65–9, 73, 74, 75, 78,
    80, 81, 82, 90, 92, 101–6,
    108, 110–13, 116–21, 123,
    130, 131, 138, 145, 148, 150,
    155, 156, 159, 160, 161, 166,
    168, 169, 171, 172, 173
  content aggregator 118
  content creation 18, 25
  content delivery 8, 9, 16, 17,
    21, 44, 46, 47, 55, 66–9,
    105, 113, 118, 148
  content description 47, 103
  Content Encryption Key
    (CEK) 103
  Content Issuer **102**, 104

content provider 14, 15, 16, 62,
 72, 73, 101, 112, 116, 117,
 118, 121, 123, 130, 161,
 171, 173
content provision 25, 27
general content distribution **66**
push of DRM Content **104**
streaming of DRM Content
 104
Coral Consortium 113
Customer 2, 4, 12, 15, 45, 51, 59,
 101, 120, 122, 123, 124, 126,
 131, 145, 153, 157, 161,
 169, 173
customer database 120, 122
customer feedback 146, 153

Datacast 42, 115, 118, 119, 120,
 121, 138, 141, 142
Decoding 27, 36, 37
Decryption 109
Delivery 7, 8, 9, 15, 16, 17, 18,
 20, 29, 42, 47, 61, 68, 73, 74,
 89, 113, 129, 134, 141, 142,
 153, 164, 171, 173
content delivery, *see* Content
data delivery 6, 7, 8, 9, 59, 60,
 65, 88
file delivery, *see* File
multimedia delivery, *see*
 Multimedia
real-time delivery 9
reliable delivery 8
Demodulation 32
Dial-up 11
Digital Audio Broadcasting (DAB)
 78, 79, 80, 81, 82, 88, 98,
 134, 136
Digital Multimedia Broadcasting
 (DMB) 71, **78–88**, 97, 98,
 132, 133, 134, 172
Satellite Digital Multimedia
 Broadcasting (S-DMB) 71,
 79, 98

Terrestrial Digital Multimedia
 Broadcasting (T-DMB) 71,
 79, 98, 136
Digital Rights Management (DRM)
 3, 17, 26, 50, 67, 101, 102,
 104, 110, 112, 113, 117,
 118, 130
DRM Agent **102**, 103, 104
DRM Content 102, 103, 104
DRM Content Format (DCF)
 103
OMA DRM **102–4**
Windows Media DRM **105–6**
Digital Video Broadcasting (DVB)
 27, **28–39**, 77, 78, 98
Digital Video Broadcasting
 Cable (DVB-C) 29
Digital Video Broadcasting
 Handheld (DVB-H) 24,
 26, 27, 29, **30–9**, 40, 43,
 46, 48, 56, 59, 65, 68, 71,
 72, 74, 77, 78, 97, 98, 101,
 124, 127, 132–7, 141, 142,
 143, 145–50, 171, 172
DVB-H receiver **32**, 127, 128
DVB-H signaling 38
DVB-H trials, *see* Trial
Digital Video Broadcasting
 Satellite (DVB-S) 29
Digital Video Broadcasting
 Terrestrial (DVB-T)
 29–30, 31, 32, 37, 38, 136
DVB Conditional Access
 (DVB-CA) **111**
DVB–Convergence of Broadcast
 and Mobile Services
 (DVB-CBMS) 27
Direct Methanol Fuel Cell
 (DMFC) 126
Doppler effect 29, 31, 36, **135**
Downlink 8, 16, 21, 49, 105,
 164, 168
Dynamic membership **11**

Early adopter 162
Early majority 162
E-commerce 66, 120
EDGE, *see* Enhanced Data rates for GSM Evolution
Electronic Program Guide (EPG) 40, 90
Electronic Service Guide (ESG) 24, 25, 26, 30, **40–3**, 46, 48, 59, 119, 156
  ESG acquisition 41
  ESG bootstrap 41
  ESG update 41
Elementary Stream (ES) 30, 34, 35, 36
Encapsulating Security Payload (ESP) 107, 108
Encryption 14, 30, 73, 105, 106, 109, 112, 113, 132
  Advanced Encryption Standard (AES) 109
  Content Encryption Key (CEK) **103**
  Rights Encryption Key (REK) **104**
Enhanced Data rates for GSM Evolution (EDGE) 2, 49, 55
Entertainment 66, 116, 123, 128, 129, 160, 161, 162
European Commission (EC) 136, 137
European Telecommunications Standards Institute (ETSI) 29, 78
Event Detail Record (EDR) 131

F8-mode 109
Fast Information Channel (FIC) **84**
Federal Communications Commission (FCC) 134, 136
File 2, 18, 42, 47, 80, 81, 105, 112
  file delivery 24, 46, 47, 48

File Delivery Table 47
file downloading 8, 40, 64, 66
file downloading service 65
Filecast **18**
File Delivery over Unidirectional Transport (FLUTE) 27, 28, 42, **47**, 48, 66
Flat rate 15, 130
Forward Error Correction (FEC) 22, 31, 32, 48
Forward Error Correction for Multiprotocol Encapsulated data (MPE-FEC) 31, 32, **36–7**, 38
Forward Link Only (FLO) 71–8, 134, 150
  FLO's air interface 73, 74, 75
Frequency 28, 31, 50, 73, 77, 79, 86, 87, 90, 98, 119, 132, 133, 135, 137, 148
  frequency diversity 74
  frequency interleaving, *see* Interleaving
Fun 161
Function 2, 11, 14, 60, 61, 62, 64, 75, 105, 109, 124, 126, 130
  cost function 11
  key derivation function 109
  membership function **61**, 64
  proxy and transport function 61, **62**, 64
  security function 61, **63**
  service announcement function 61, **62–3**
  session and transmission function **61**
Functional entity 25, 26, 102
Functional group 42

General Packet Radio Service (GPRS) 2, 49, 146, 148
  GPRS Gateway Support Node (GGSN) 61–4

GPRS Tunneling Protocol
(GTP)   61
Global Positioning System (GPS)   2
Global System for Mobile
communications (GSM)   5,
49, 55, 60, 133, 135, 168
GSM EDGE Radio Access
Network (GERAN)   55,
60, 61
Gmb   63, 64
Guard interval   29, 30, 86, 92, 93

H.263   45, 146, 148
H.264   30, 45, 73, 82, 98,
146, 148
Handover   21, 31, 35, 36, 49,
57, 79
active handover   21
seamless handover   31, 32,
34, 36
Handset   49, 115, 122, 123, 124,
128, 129, 138, 149, 160
handset subsidies   122
Hierarchical transmission   90, 92,
93, 94, 97
High Definition Television
(HDTV)   28, 90, 97
High Speed Downlink Packet
Access (HSDPA)   49, 56

In-depth interleaver   32, 37–8
Indoor   29, 31, 90, 129, 146, 148,
158, 160
Innovator   162
Integrated Services Digital
Broadcasting (ISDB)   88, 89
Integrated Services Digital
Broadcasting Cable
(ISDB-C)   88, 97
Integrated Services Digital
Broadcasting Satellite
(ISDB-S)   88, 89, 97

Integrated Services Digital
Broadcasting Terrestrial
(ISDB-T)   28, 71, **88–97**, 98
Integrity   106, 108, 109, 110
data integrity   15, 107, 110
Interaction   26, 27, 62, 166,
167, 168
interaction channel, see Channel
Interleaving   38, 84, 93
bit interleaving   94
frequency interleaving   92,
93, 94
time interleaving   28, 84,
92, 93
International Telecommunication
Union (ITU)   82, 133, 136
ITU Radiocommunication Sector
(ITU-R)   133, 136
ITU Telecommunication
Standardization Sector
(ITU-T)   49
Internet   2, 5, 20, 23, 50, 61, 65,
73, 80, 90, 131, 132
Internet Group Management
Protocol (IGMP)   14
Internet Protocol (IP)   17, 19,
24, 25, 27, 28, 31–4, 36,
37, 40, 44–7, 49, 71, 73,
77, 80, 81, 88, 106, 108,
115, 118, 119, 120,
141, 142
IP multicast, see Multicast
IPv4   15
IPv6   15
Internet Protocol Datacasting
(IPDC)   3, 16, **23–53**, 101,
106, 107, 108, 110, 111,
115, 116, 118, 119, 120,
123, 124, 127, 141, 142,
171, 172, 173
Internet Protocol security (IPsec)
14, **106–8**, 148
Internet Service Provider
(ISP)   12

Internet (*Continued*)
 Internet Streaming Media
  Alliance Encryption and
  Authentication
  (ISMACrypt) **110–11**

Keyed-Hashing for Message
 Authentication, *see*
 Authentication
Key Stream Layer 108
Key Stream Message (KSM) 107
Killer application 3, 173

Laggard/rejecter 162
Late majority 162
Layered Coding Transport (LCT)
 28, 48
Loss 8, 14, 22, 60, 64, 65, 105,
 108, 135
 penetration loss 135
 propagation loss 135

Main Service Channel (MSC)
 80, **84**
Management 12, 13, 14, 15, 16,
 26, 56, 60, 73, 109, 110, 111,
 133, 137
 group management 14
 network management 14, 56
 service management 26
Marketing 66, 67, 122
Market research 4
MBMS, *see* Multimedia
 Broadcast/Multicast Service
Media discovery 18
MediaFLO **71–8**, 97, 98, 134,
 141, 142, 150, 151
Membership function, *see* Function
Mhealth 10, 11
Mobile phone 23, 48, 78, 88,
 114, 123, 127, 129, 146, 155,
 166, 169, 173
Mobility **21–2**, 31, 37, 60, 64
Mobisode 116

Modulation 28, 29, 30, 37,
 75, 86, 87, 90, 92, 93, 94,
 96, 97
 layered modulation **74**,
  77, 150
 multicarrier modulation 86
Moving Picture Experts Group
 (MPEG) 82, 110
 MPEG-1 81
 MPEG-2 27, 30, 32, 33,
  34, 43–6, 81, 88, 89, 90,
  92, 93
 MPEG-4 82
Multi-access link 11
Multicast 2, 3, 5, 6, 7, 8–13,
 15–21, 47, 56–9, 61, 62, 63,
 66–9, 71, 77, 97, 108, 112,
 121, 141, 148, 153, 154, 164,
 168, 171, 173
 active multicast 8, 9
 application layer multicast 7
 IP multicast 5, 14, 15, **16–22**,
  59, 61
 multicast gain 12
 multicast group 10, 11, 14,
  57, 59
 Multicast Health Monitor 10
 multicast service 18, 19,
  21, 57, 61, 62, 66, 67,
  142, 157
  multicast service area 57
 multicast tree 10, 11, 15
 multicast tunnel **10**
 network layer multicast 7, 8
 passive multicast 8, 9
 physical layer multicast 7
 routed multicast 20
 tunneled multicast 20
Multi Frequency Network (MFN)
 79, 87, 98
Multimedia 1, 8, 23, 56, 57, 78,
 112, 126, 129
 multimedia content 3, 80,
  113

multimedia delivery   5, 97, 98,
    141, 154
Multimedia Messaging System
    (MMS)   23, 50, 51, 67
Multimedia Object Transfer
    (MOT)   80
multimedia service   2, 6, 9, 23,
    25, 28, 55, 65, 97, 121,
    126, 133, 137, 142, 150,
    153, 154, 171
Multimedia Broadcast/Multicast
    Service (MBMS)   3, 16, 55–69,
    71, 97, 98, 101, 115, 116,
    118, 119, 120–3, 132, 141,
    142, 149, 150, 171, 172, 173
MBMS Bearer Context   63, 64
MBMS services   55, 58, 60, 61,
    65–8, 118, 121, 122, 123
MBMS trials, see Trial
MBMS UE Context   64
Multiplex Configuration
    Information (MCI)   84, 86
Multipoint-to-multipoint   7, 67
Multipoint-to-point   7
Multiprotocol Encapsulation
    (MPE)   31, 34, 36, 38, 43,
    44, 45
    MPE-FEC, see Forward Error
        Correction for
        Multiprotocol Encapsulated
        data

Network   2, 5–9, 11, 12, 13, 14,
    15, 16, 19, 21, 23, 26, 27, 30,
    31, 33, 34, 37, 49, 55, 56, 57,
    59, 60, 61, 64, 65, 68, 69, 73,
    79, 80, 86, 87, 97, 98, 105,
    108, 109, 112, 117, 118, 120,
    121, 123–6, 132, 141, 142,
    145, 146, 148, 149, 150, 153,
    154, 168, 169, 172, 173
access network   16, 172
broadcast network   6, 24, 26,
    27, 28, 43, 48, 50, 51, 56,

    65, 78, 97, 105, 111, 115,
    120, 124, 172
cellular network   2, 3, 16, 48–51,
    55, 77, 97, 101, 115, 117,
    120, 121, 124, 125, 129,
    132, 133, 168, 172, 173
core network   5, 16, 56, 57, 59
interactive network   26
mobile network   23, 60, 61,
    109, 120, 122, 142
network heterogeneity   125
network layer   44, 47, 80
network management, see
    Management
network operator   16, 18, 23,
    120, 130, 158, 159, 169
    cellular network operator   55,
        115, 118, 120, 121, 173
    datacast network operator
        119, 120, 121, 138
    mobile network operator
        120, 150
network provider   9
television (TV) network   28, 88
News clips   66
Node-B   59
Non-program-associated data
    (NPAD)   80
NULL cipher   109

Open Mobile Alliance (OMA)
    102, 104
    OMA DRM, see Digital Rights
        Management
Operations center
    Local Operations Center
        (LOC)   72
    National Operations Center
        (NOC)   72
    Network Operations Center
        72, 73
    Service Operation Center
        (SOC)   42

Orthogonal Frequency Division
Multiplexing (OFDM) 28,
29, 31, 32, 71, 77, 86, 87, 90,
92, 93, 94, 96, 97
OFDM modulation block
93, 94
OSI/ISO layer model 24, 74, 75
Outdoor 29, 31, 90, 158
Overhead Information Symbols
(OIS) 75

Pay-per-content 14, 122, 130
Pay-per-download 118
Pay-per-duration 130
Pay-per-view 1, 122, 130
Peer-to-peer 166, 168
Personal Digital Assistant (PDA)
88, 127, 146
Picture quality 155
Podcast 161
Point-to-multipoint (PTMP) 2, 3,
7, 9, 16, 55, 56, 57, 59, 121
Point-to-point 2, 5, 6, 7, 9, 11, 16,
18, 57, 59, 63, 121, 141, 173
Portable 2, 28, 29, 30, 105
portable intelligence 124, 125
Power consumption 23, 30, 31,
32, 59, 74, 76, 86, 126
Power control 59
Prepaid 122, 131, 148
Preview 59, 102, 106, 121
Program-associated data
(PAD) 81
Program Specific
Information/Service
Information (PSI/SI) 28

Quality of service (QoS) 2, 15,
17, 64, 65, 74, 82, 125, 135

Radio Access Network (RAN)
55, 57
Radio spectrum 2, **132–7**

Radio Spectrum Committee
(RSC) 136
Radio Spectrum Decision 136
Radio Spectrum Policy Group
(RSPG) 136, 137
Real-Time Control Protocol
(RTCP) 10, 17, 28, 44, 108
Real-Time Streaming Protocol
(RTSP) 17, 110
Real-Time Transport Protocol
(RTP) 16, 17, 28, 44, 45,
108, 109, 110
Re-broadcasting 166
Reception 28, 29, 31, 35–8, 44,
57, 59, 63, 69, 74, 79, 84, 89,
90, 97, 127, 129, 135, 141,
145, 146, 148, 149, 156,
158, 159
partial reception 90, 93, 94, 97
unauthorized reception 14
Reed-Solomon (RS) 36, 37, 76,
92, 93
Reference
reference model 16, 17
reference point 63
Reliability 8, 16, 17, 18, 65, 76,
82, 141
Reliable Multicast Transport
(RMT) 18
Replay 106, 108, 110
Rights 13, 18, 43, 101, 102, 105,
120, 137
Rights Encryption Key (REK),
see Encryption
Rights Issuer 42, **102**, 103, 104
Rights Management Layer
108, 110
Rights Object **102**, 103,
104, 108

Satellite Digital Multimedia
Broadcasting (S-DMB), see
Digital Multimedia
Broadcasting

Screencast 161
Secure Real-Time Transport
    Protocol (SRTP) **108–10**
Security 8, 13, 14, 15, 18, 25, 26,
    27, 61, 63, 106–10, 112, 117,
    132, 148
  Security Association (SA) 106,
    107, 108
  Security Parameter Index
    (SPI) 108
Segmented integer counter
    mode 109
Service 1, 2, 4, 5, 6, 8, 9, 12–18,
    21, 23, 25–34, 36, 38, 40–3,
    45–50, 51, 55–67, 71, 72, 73,
    75–82, 84, 86, 88, 89, 90, 93,
    97, 101, 106, 113, 115,
    117–25, 127–38, 141–5,
    153–9, 161–9, 171, 172, 173
  announcement service 67
  audio and video clip service **66**
  broadcast service, *see* Broadcast
  carousel service **65–6**
  file downloading service, *see* File
  interactive service 2, 90, 120,
    168, 169
  localized service **66**
  MBMS service, *see* Multimedia
    Broadcast/Multicast Service
    (MBMS)
  multicast service, *see* Multicast
  multimedia service, *see*
    Multimedia
  multipoint-to-multipoint service
    67
  point-to-multipoint service 3
  service announcement 18, 58,
    59, 60–3
  Service Application 25, 26
  service area 31, 56, 57, 60, 62
  service availability 57, 129, 155
  Service Configuration 26
  service convergence 124
  service discovery 31, 38

Service Guide Provisioning
    Application 26
Service Level Agreement
    (SLA) 16
Service Management 26
service neutrality 137
Service Operation Center (SOC),
    see Operations center
Service Protection Provision 26
service provider 9, 14, 59, 61,
    101, 105, 118, 119, 120,
    121, 132, 136, 169
service provisioning 58, 61
service usage 9, 158, 159
service value chain, *see* Value
    chain
Short Message Service (SMS)
    49, 63, 131, 146
  premium SMS 130–1
  streaming service 48, 65, 66,
    71, 142, 148, 168, 169
  subscription-based service 105,
    106, 121
Serving GPRS Support Node
    (SGSN) 60, 61, 64
Session Announcement Protocol
    (SAP) 18
Session Description Protocol (SDP)
    18, 43, 110
Signaling 8, 12, 19, 21, 28, 32,
    38, 62, 63, 64
  DVB-H signaling, *see* Digital
    Video Broadcasting
Signal-to-Interference Ratio
    (SIR) 59
Signal-to-Noise Ratio (SNR) 74
Single Frequency Network (SFN)
    30, 31, 33, 37, 71, 79, 86, 87,
    90, 97, 98, 150, 153
Smart-phone 126
Software 47, 50, 66, 68, 112,
    123, 130, 138, 172

Software (*Continued*)
   software vendor   16, 115, 123,
      129, 130
Spectrum   30, 50, 78, 90, 97,
      98, **132–7**, 145, 146, 149,
      150, 155
   radio spectrum, *see* Radio
      spectrum
   spectrum allocation   132, 133,
      135, 136, 137, 138
   spectrum auction   136
   spectrum commercialization
      137
   spectrum harmonization   132,
      136, 137
   spectrum management   137
Standardization   3, 78, 132, 133
Storage   17, 76, 124
   off-device storage   **103**
Streaming   17, 23, 28, **43–5**, 46,
      48, 49, 55, 56, 64, 65, 66, 74,
      76, 78, 80, 97, 104, 118,
      146, 172
   streaming class   64, 65
   streaming service, *see* Service
Subcasting   16
Subscription   18, 43, 57, **59**, 66,
      67, 73, 101, 105, 106,
      118–21, 130, 162
Subtitle   48, 128, 147, 155
Success factor   124, 156
Superdistribution   **102**, 104
Super-frame   75, 76
Sweet spot   12

TDtv   149
Teaser   59
Technology neutrality   137
Television (TV)   2, 3, 16, 24, 27,
      28, 29, 40, 43, 45, 65, 66, 71,
      79, 81, 88, 89, 90, 98, 120,
      132, 133, 146, 147, 150, 156,
      157, 160, 164, 165, 166, 168,
      171, 172, 173

mobile television (TV)   3, 17,
      56, 78, 79, 84, 88, 97, 116,
      122, 129, 132, 133, 135–8,
      142, 145, 148, 150, 153–7,
      160–9, 171, 173
   pay-TV   148
   terrestrial television   6, 28, 88,
      136, 156, 159
Terminal   1, 2, 5, 21, 26, 27,
      29, 30–3, 37, 40, 41, 56, 57,
      59, 65, 67, 68, 72, 73, 74,
      76, 77, 82, 101, 105, 108,
      122, **123–30**, 141, 146, 147,
      149, 150, 155, 157, 160, 161,
      162, 164, 165, 166, 168, 171,
      172, 173
   terminal convergence   124
   terminal heterogeneity   **125**
Terrestrial   29, 71, 78, 79, 87, 88,
      89, 165, 166, 172
   Digital Video Broadcasting
      Terrestrial (DVB-T),
      see Digital Video
      Broadcasting
   Terrestrial Digital Multimedia
      Broadcasting (T-DMB), *see*
      Digital Multimedia
      Broadcasting
   Terrestrial Integrated Services
      Digital Broadcasting
      (ISDB-T), *see* Integrated
      Services Digital
      Broadcasting
   terrestrial television, *see*
      Television
Threat   14, 153, **155–6**
Time Division Multiple Access
      (TDMA)   49
Time Division Multiplexing (TDM)
      74, 75
Time interleaving, *see*
      Interleaving
Time slicing   26, 31, 32,
      34–6, 38

Transmission and Multiplexing Configuration Control (TMCC) 97
Transmission quality 155
Transmitter Parameter Signaling (TPS) 31, 38
Trial 4, 71, 78, 79, 130, 141–51, 153, 154, 156–60
DVB-H trials 142–8
MBMS trials 149–50
MediaFLO trials 150–1

Ultra High Frequency (UHF) 98, 132, 135
Ultra Lightweight Encapsulation (ULE) 44
Unicast 5, 6, 7, 9, 10, 11, 13, 15, 20, 77, 108, 133, 142, 157
Universal Mobile Telecommunications System (UMTS) 5, 23, 50, 55, 59, 60, 64, 98, 109, 133, 142, 150; 168
UMTS Terrestrial Radio Access Network (UTRAN) 55, 56, 59, 60, 61
Uplink 21, 26, 27, 72, 73, 98, 146
uplink channel 8, 21, 24, 48, 67, 105, 148, 168, 173
Usage 5, 7, 9, 15, 23, 30, 49, 55, 64, 69, 74, 77, 97, 101, 102, 104, 112, 121, 122, 137, 153, 154, 155, 158, 159, 160, 164, 166
service usage, see Service
usage report 8
usage scheme 158–61
User 1, 2, 3, 5–9, 13, 14, 16, 18, 19, 21, 25, 26, 28, 31, 34, 40–3, 45, 50, 51, 55–65, 67, 73, 76, 78, 82, 101, 103, 104, 105, 106, 112, 113, 116–22,

124, 125, 126, 129, 130, 131, 133, 135, 142, 145, 151, 153–60, 161–3, 164, 168, 169, 171, 172, 173
end user 9, 14, 30, 56, 80, 122, 171, 172
user attitude 141, 153, 159
user-centric interface 124, 125
user experience 2, 124
user feedback 141, 145, 153–70, 173
user friendliness 125
user interface 71, 123, 130
user-network communication 8
active user-network communication 8
passive user-network communication 8
user personalization 125
User Datagram Protocol (UDP) 28, 44, 46, 47

Value chain 27, 115, 116, 119, 122, 130, 138, 148
Videoconferencing 8, 67
Video-on-demand (VoD) 1, 45, 50, 105, 117, 120
Video quality 127, 147, 155, 156
Viterbi decoder 84

Wideband Code Division Multiple Access (WCDMA), see Code Division Multiple Access
WiFi 133, 172
WiMAX 133, 172
Windows Media DRM, see Digital Rights Management
Wireless Access Policy for Electronic Communications Services (WAPECS) 137
World Administrative Radio Conference (WARC) 136